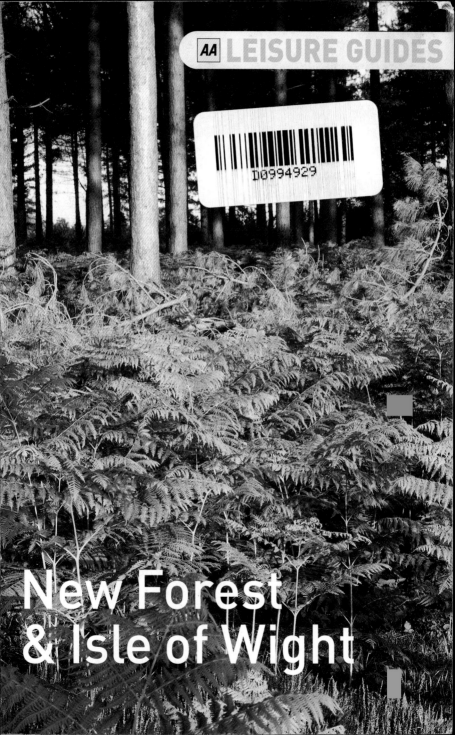

AA LEISURE GUIDES

D0994929

New Forest
& Isle of Wight

Authors: Helen Livingston and Ann F Stonehouse
Verifier: Ann F Stonehouse
Publisher: David Watchus
Managing Editor: Katey Mackenzie
Senior Editors: Isla Love and Sheila Hawkins
Senior Designers: Alison Fenton and Kat Mead
Page Layout: Andrew Milne Design
Picture Library Manager: Liz Allen
Picture Research: Alice Earle
Cartographic Editor: Jenny Wood of Skelley Cartographic Services
Cartographic Production: Geoff Chapman, Samantha Chalkley-Johnston and Graham Jones
Copy-editors: Marilynne Lanng of Bookwork and Pamela Stagg
Proofreader: Sheila Hawkins
Index: Hilary Bird
Internal Repro: Sarah Butler, Ian Little and Michael Moody

Produced by AA Publishing
© Automobile Association Developments Limited 2007

Published by AA Publishing (a trading name of Automobile Association Developments Limited, whose
registered office is Fanum House, Basing View, Basingstoke, Hampshire RG21 4EA; registered number
1878835).

 This product includes mapping data licensed from the Ordnance Survey® with the
permission of the Controller of Her Majesty's Stationery Office.
© Crown copyright 2007. All rights reserved. Licence number 399221.

A03033

ISBN-10: 0-7495-5016-3
ISBN-13: 978-0-7495-5016-5

A CIP catalogue record for this book is available from the British Library.

The contents of this book are believed correct at the time of printing. Nevertheless, the publishers
cannot be held responsible for any errors or omissions or for changes in the details given in this book
or for the consequences of any reliance on the information it provides. We have tried to ensure
accuracy in this book, but things do change and would be grateful if readers would advise us of any
inaccuracies they may encounter. This does not affect your statutory rights.

We have taken all reasonable steps to ensure that the walks and cycle rides in this book are safe and
achievable by people with a realistic level of fitness. However, all outdoor activities involve a degree of
risk and the publishers accept no responsibility for any injuries caused to readers whilst following
these walks and cycle rides. For advice on walking and cycling in safety, see pages 16–17.

Some of the walks and cycle rides may appear in other AA books and publications.

Visit AA Publishing's website www.theAA.com/travel

Colour reproduction by Keenes Group, Andover
Printed by C & C Offset Printers, China

CONTENTS

INTRODUCTION 6

EAST DORSET 18
■ WALKS 1 & 2 ■ CAR TOUR 1

NEW FOREST 48
■ WALKS 3, 4 & 5 ■ CYCLE RIDES 1 & 2

ISLE OF WIGHT 82
■ WALK 6 ■ CYCLE RIDE 3

PORTSMOUTH & SOUTHEAST COAST 106
■ WALKS 7 & 8

WINCHESTER & SALISBURY 126
■ WALKS 9 & 10 ■ CAR TOUR 2

INFORMATION: WALKS & CYCLE RIDES 16

USEFUL INFORMATION 152

ATLAS 153

INDEX & ACKNOWLEDGEMENTS 158

Welcome to the...

New Forest
& Isle of Wight

INTRODUCTION

This beautiful region includes some of the best of rural Hampshire, Wiltshire and Dorset, with many of the South's prettiest villages and most appealing small towns thrown in for good measure. It takes in some of its biggest conurbations, too – sprawling cities such as Southampton, Portsmouth and Bournemouth, with historic hearts of gold.

As an area to explore, it simply has to include the Isle of Wight, which remains an entire world of its own, slightly apart from the 21st century. The New Forest, famed for its wildlife conservation and natural beauty, is one of Britain's newest national parks, a status that helps to preserve ancient traditions of land management, and has meant better access than ever for walkers and cyclists. And it would be absurd not to venture along the coast to the chalky Jurassic cliffs of east Dorset, celebrated as a World Heritage

Site. Inland there are the winding streams of rural Hampshire to discover, and historic Winchester with its squat, medieval cathedral and Jane Austen links. From here, cross into Wiltshire to the busy market town of Salisbury, with its soaring Gothic cathedral, or to link the two at Romsey, where a massive Norman abbey completes the trio of architectural gems.

If you enjoy stately homes and museums, some of the best in the South are here, including the National Motor Museum at Beaulieu, the Historic Ships collection at Portsmouth, and grand mansions such as Wilton House, Kingston Lacey, Osborne, and the famous gardens of Exbury and Mottisfont Abbey. There are glorious, golden sandy beaches at Studland, Swanage and Bournemouth, and inland the superb downs, ancient woodland and open heath to discover. There is something for everyone in this diverse region.

■ FRESHWATER BAY

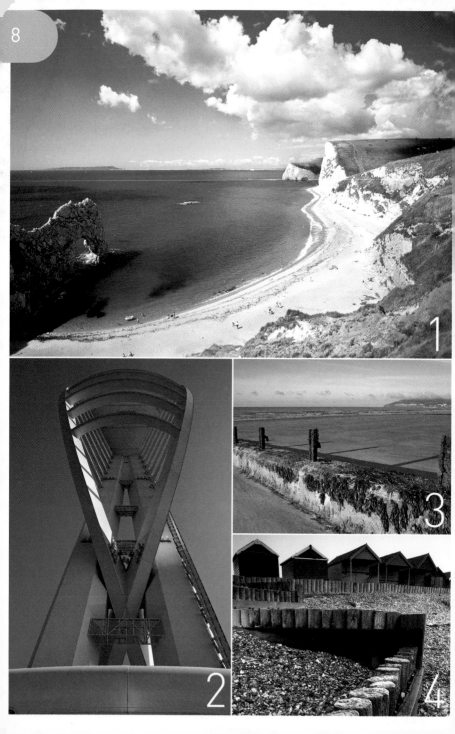

ESSENTIAL SPOTS

If you have little time and you want to sample the essence of the New Forest and its coastline: Picnic under a canvass of ancient oaks deep in the forest...join the boating fraternity and sail out of Lymington...visit atmospheric Osborne House...clamber aboard and imagine life on Nelson's flagship HMS *Victory*...dance the night away in the many bars and clubs of trendy Bournemouth...sunbathe on Studland's beautiful sandy beach...walk among the eery jagged ruins of Corfe Castle... enjoy a gentle train ride on busy Alresford's Watercress Line...listen to the choir sing and admire the stained-glass windows in Winchester Cathedral.

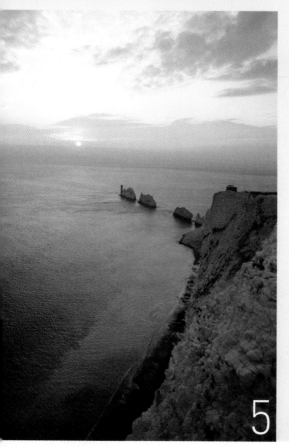

5

1 Lulworth Cove/ Durdle Door

Crescent shaped Lulworth Cove is a popular spot now for holiday-makers. Its towering limestone cliffs hold the secrets of its history – fossils that tell of a time when dinosaurs wandered the earth, and before, when this part of the south coast was deep under the sea.

2 Spinnaker Tower

Portsmouth's Spinnaker Tower was the city's main millennium project. It was planned to open in 2000, but the tower opened to its waiting public in 2005. The tourist attraction stands 558 feet (170m) high and the viewing platform at the top can be reached by a choice of high-speed or panoramic lifts.

3 Sandown

Since the Victorian era, this gently shelving beach on the Isle of Wight has been popular with holiday-makers and families.

4 Calshot

Colourful, traditional seaside huts are a sign of a long-established beach and this is true of Calshot. It is mostly pebbly underfoot.

5 The Needles

These limestone stacks have long been a welcome sight for weary sailors but many ships have foundered on these dangerous rocks.

New Forest Ponies
6 These friendly horses have roamed free on their ancient homeland of heath and woods for centuries.

Shanklin Chine
7 A chine is a deep ravine, formed here as water has carved out a narrow path through the stone below. The waterfall is a feature of this lovely area that is known for its variety of wildlife and range of flora.

Christchurch
8 The Avon and the Stour meet at this popular town. The riverfront is dominated by moored craft of varying sizes and condition and there is invariably someone painting or renovating their boat moored here. The river itself is always busy with pleasure craft on tours of the area, and serious sailors heading out to, or returning from, the sea.

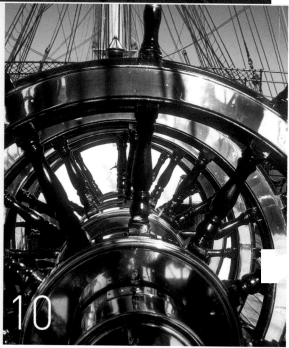

9 Studland
Long and sandy South beach, Studland, stretches back to hilly dunes and heathland – a national nature reserve – good for interesting treks. The more northern end of the beach is used by naturists. If you are approaching Studland from Poole, take the ferry and enjoy the short journey across the mouth of Poole Harbour.

10 HMS *Warrior*
Launched in 1860, HMS *Warrior* was one of the fastest vessels of its day, powered by both steam and sail. *Warrior's* gleaming decks can be seen in Portsmouth.

DAY ONE

For many people a weekend break or a long weekend is a popular way of spending their leisure time. These four pages offer a loosely planned itinerary designed to ensure that you make the most of your time, what ever the weather, and see and enjoy the very best the area has to offer.

Friday Night

Spoil yourself with an overnight stay at the Rhinefield House Hotel, which lies off the A35 southwest of Lyndhurst. It's a Victorian pastiche of a grand Elizabethan mansion, set in several acres of lovely landscaped Italian-style grounds. Relax in the opulent lounge before entering the grand dining hall for dinner – the menu shows French influence, and there's an extensive wine list.

Saturday Morning

After a satisfying breakfast, head into the popular and busy town of Lyndhurst, the so-called 'capital' of the New Forest. Call in at the tourist office beside the main car park and select your area for a morning's walk, or hire a bicycle and follow one of the many waymarked routes. It's by far the best way to see the Forest up close. Don't forget to call in at the Serpentarium, for a sighting of this region's more unusual reptiles.

Saturday Lunch

After your morning's exertions, pick a good country pub for lunch. You're almost spoilt for choice in this region, but the Royal Oak at Fritham offers a special sort of rural simplicity, and the Trusty Servant at Minstead is always popular, offering a wide range of snacks and full meals.

Saturday Afternoon

After lunch, head west along any of the main routes (the A31–A348–A3049 is probably the least congested), and turn off the A35 at Lytchett Minster for the Isle of Purbeck. Head south, via old Wareham, then pick up the minor road, the B3070, heading down past Lulworth Castle and through Lulworth village to the almost perfect circle of Lulworth Bay. It is worth calling in to the visitor centre here for information about the local geology and fossils, before heading off on a bracing stroll along the cliff path. If it's at all damp underfoot it can be extremely slippery, and walking boots are recommended.

Saturday Evening

As evening settles in, meander through the narrow, winding country lanes to Corfe Castle and beautiful Studland, with its long sandy beach. Cross to Sandbanks on the ferry, and pick out a hotel that most appeals to you – the Harbour Heights, on Haven Road, is a great choice: recently refurbished and chic, it offers fabulous sunset views over Poole harbour from its lovely brasserie terrace, and a stylish, contemporary menu to match.

CORFE CASTLE

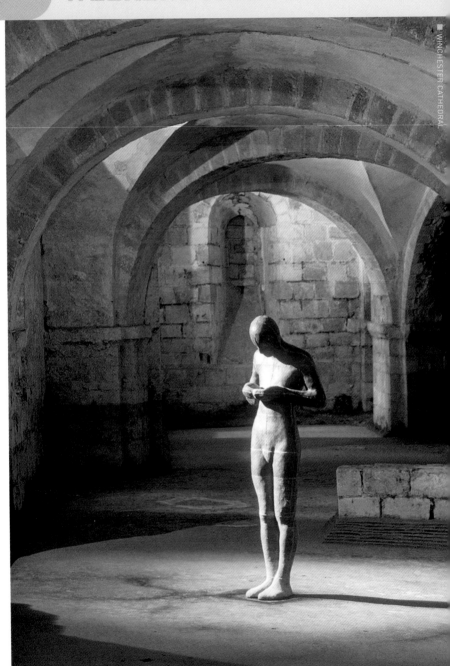

WINCHESTER CATHEDRAL

DAY TWO

Our second and final day starts with a visit to the historic port and university town of Portsmouth, with its longstanding importance to the Royal Navy, before driving inland up to the Test Valley and through the market towns of Romsey and Stockbridge on the way to Winchester. End the weekend in this cathedral town that has both ancient monuments and modern restaurants.

Sunday Morning

After an early breakfast, head northeast from Poole, via Ringwood, on the A31, and follow the M27 east to junction 7. From here, follow the A334 through the attractive old market towns of Botley and Wickham. Head south on the A32, then follow the A27 eastwards through Portchester and follow the tourist signs south to visit the historic ships collection in Portsmouth. It's unmissable, with a guided tour of Lord Nelson's flagship, HMS Victory, the highlight. If you can fit it in, the water-borne tour of the harbour, including views of the ultra-modern Spinnaker Tower, is a must.

Sunday Lunch

You could easily spend the whole day in Portsmouth, but if you want to explore the area further then drive back towards Southampton on the A27. Call in at the village of Hamble or Bursledon for lunch at a traditional waterside pub, and watch the Sunday sailors exercising their craft on the river, with a range of craft from streamlined luxury motor launches to humble dinghies.

Sunday Afternoon

Return to the M27 and head west, soon turning off at Junction 3 to visit ancient Romsey. Stroll around the town centre and explore the historic abbey, then continue northwards up the A3057 to the venerable town of Stockbridge. A fly-fisherman's delight, Stockbridge has the trout-filled River Test running through it. Enjoy a cup of tea here and perhaps some shopping along the high street, before heading east into Winchester on the B3049.

Sunday Night

There's a great choice of eating places in Winchester, as you'll discover on a pleasant stroll around the town centre when most of the visitors have gone for the evening. The elegant Hotel du Vin on Southgate offers cosy, top-notch dining in a friendly setting, and rooms behind avoid the worst of the town's traffic noise – it's a deservedly popular choice, so book ahead.

Route facts

MINIMUM TIME The time stated for completing each route is the estimated minimum time that a reasonably fit family group of walkers or cyclists would take to complete the circuit. This does not allow for rest or refreshment stops.

OS MAP Each route is shown on a map. However, some detail is lost because of the restrictions imposed by scale, so for this reason, we recommend that you use the maps in conjunction with a more detailed Ordnance Survey map. The relevant map for each walk or cycle ride is listed.

START This indicates the start location and parking area. This is a six-figure grid reference prefixed by two letters showing which 62.5-mile (100km) square of the National Grid it refers to. You'll find more information on grid references on most Ordnance Survey maps.

CYCLE HIRE We list, within reason, the nearest cycle hire shop/centre.

❶ Here we highlight any potential difficulties or dangers along the cycle ride or walk. If a particular route is suitable for older, fitter children we say so here. Also, we give guidelines of a route's suitability for younger children, for example the symbol 8+ indicates that the route can probably be attempted by children aged 8 years and above.

Walks & Cycle Rides

Each walk and cycle ride has a panel giving information for the walker and cyclist, including the distance, terrain, nature of the paths, and where to park your car.

WALKING

All of the walks are suitable for families, but less experienced family groups, especially those with younger children, should try the shorter walks. Route finding is usually straightforward, but the maps are for guidance only and we recommend that you always take the relevant Ordnance Survey map with you.

Risks

Although each walk has been researched with a view to minimising any risks, no walk in the countryside can be considered to be completely free from risk. Walking in the outdoors will always require a degree of common sense and judgement to ensure that it is as safe as possible, especially for young children.
• Be particularly careful on cliff paths and in upland terrain, where the consequences of a slip can be serious.
• Remember to check tidal conditions before walking on the seashore.
• Some sections of route are by, or cross, busy roads.

Remember traffic is a danger even on minor country lanes.
• Be careful around farmyard machinery and livestock.
• Be prepared for the consequences of changes in the weather and check the forecast before you set out.
• Ensure the whole family is properly equipped, wearing suitable clothing and a good pair of boots or sturdy walking shoes. Take waterproof clothing with you and a torch if you are walking in the winter months.
• Remember the weather can change quickly at any time of the year, and in moorland and heathland areas, mist and fog can make route-finding much harder. In summer, take account of the heat and sun by wearing a hat, sunscreen and carrying enough water.
• On walks away from centres of population you should carry a mobile phone, whistle and, if possible, a survival bag. If you do have an accident requiring emergency services, make a note of your position as accurately as possible and dial 999.

CYCLING

In devising the cycle rides in this guide, every effort has been made to use designated cycle paths, or to link them with quiet country lanes and waymarked byways and bridleways. In a few cases, some fairly busy B-roads have been used to join up with quieter routes.

Rules of the road

• Ride in single file on narrow and busy roads.
• Be alert, look and listen for traffic, especially on narrow lanes and blind bends, and be extra careful when descending steep hills, as loose gravel or a poor road surface can lead to an accident.
• In wet weather make sure that you keep an appropriate distance between you and other riders.
• Make sure you indicate your intentions clearly.
• Brush up on *The Highway Code* before venturing out on to the road.

Off-road safety code of conduct

• Only ride where you know it is legal to do so. Cyclists are not allowed to cycle on public footpaths, marked in yellow. The only 'rights of way' open to cyclists are bridleways (blue markers) and unsurfaced tracks, known as byways, which are open to all traffic and waymarked in red.
• Canal towpaths: you need a permit to cycle on some stretches of towpath (www.waterscape.com). Remember that access paths can be steep and slippery so always push your bike under low bridges and by locks.
• Always yield to walkers and horses, giving adequate warning of your approach.
• Don't expect to cycle at high speeds.
• Keep to the main trail to avoid any unnecessary erosion to the area beside the trail and to prevent skidding, especially in wet weather conditions.
• Remember to follow the Country Code.

Preparing your bicycle

Check the wheels, tyres, brakes and cables. Lubricate hubs, pedals, gear mechanisms and cables. Make sure you have a pump, a bell, a rear rack to carry panniers and a set of lights.

Equipment

• A cycling helmet provides essential protection.
• Make sure you are visible to other road users, by wearing light-coloured or luminous clothing in daylight and sashes or reflective strips in failing light and darkness.
• Take extra clothes with you, depending on the season, and a wind/waterproof jacket.
• Carry a basic tool kit, a pump, a strong lock and a first aid kit.
• Always carry enough water for your outing.

Walk Map Legend

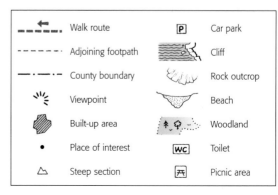

←----	Walk route	P	Car park
------	Adjoining footpath		Cliff
—·—·—	County boundary		Rock outcrop
☼	Viewpoint		Beach
	Built-up area		Woodland
•	Place of interest	WC	Toilet
△	Steep section	⊼	Picnic area

East Dorset

BOURNEMOUTH ■ BOVINGTON ■ WALK 1 ■ CORFE CASTLE

CRANBORNE CHASE ■ KIMMERIDGE BAY ■ KINGSTON LACY

LULWORTH COVE ■ MILTON ABBAS ■ POOLE ■ STUDLAND

WALK 2 ■ CAR TOUR 1 ■ SWANAGE ■ TOLPUDDLE

WAREHAM ■ WIMBORNE MINSTER

BOURNEMOUTH BEACHES

WELCOME TO BOURNEMOUTH PIER WELCOME TO

2 WAVE WRIGHT ONLY
EMERGENCY VEHICLES
ONLY

PIER THEATRE
BOOKING OFFICE

FUN FAIR
ALL RIDES STILL HERE £1.50

TRIPS
THE PIER

BOAT TRIPS
FROM THE PIER

The region of eastern Dorset incorporates a variety of pretty, pocket-size villages and towns, and a stretch of coastline that is famous for its fossil cliffs and is dubbed England's Jurassic Coast. With chalky downland, the woodland of Cranbourne Chase, the high ridges of the Purbeck Hills and the glorious golden sands of Studland and Bournemouth, there is plenty of variation in the landscape too. Follow in the footsteps of Lawrence of Arabia, Thomas Hardy and the Tolpuddle Martyrs as you explore.

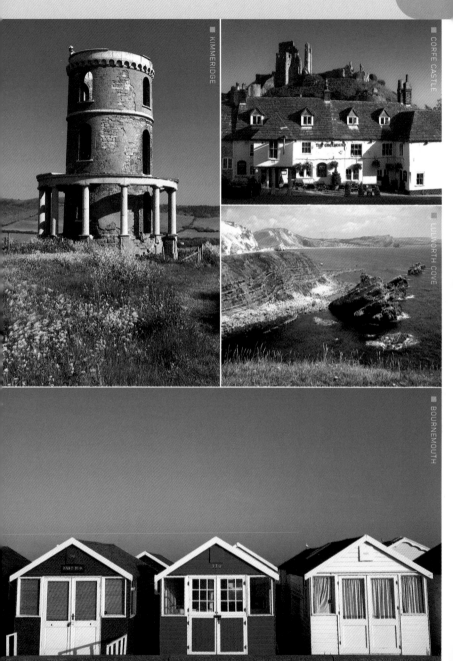

KIMMERIDGE

CORFE CASTLE

LULWORTH COVE

BOURNEMOUTH

Unmissable attractions

Walk along the golden, sandy beaches of Bournemouth or Studland...climb up to the haunting ruins of Corfe Castle...visit the grand 17th-century mansion of Kingston Lacy...marvel at the rock formations in Lulworth Cove and the stone arch of Durdle Door that sits just off its beach...take part in a nostalgic Punch and Judy show while enjoying an ice cream at the Victorian pier at Swanage...act out the part of an army commander and climb aboard an authentic tank at Bovington's fascinating Tank Museum...picnic in the rolling grasslands of Cranborne Chase surrounded by a mist of colourful butterflies...fill up on fish and chips at Poole's thriving quayside.

1 Corfe Castle
The castle was destroyed during the Civil War after a long siege. Then, the defenders were allowed to leave before the castle was damaged beyond repair, in order to prevent its further use.

2 Bournemouth Pier
The pier underwent a costly renovation in the early 1980s and is now an essential attraction along Bournemouth's seafront.

3 Lulworth Cove
Although popular with those who favour paddling and sitting by the sea, the area surrounding Lulworth Cove and Durdle Door is wonderful for anyone who prefers to walk and enjoy the variety of landscape here including open spaces and narrow, chalk paths.

4 Kingston Lacy
The wealthy Bankes family built Kingston Lacy as their new home after their family seat, Corfe Castle, was destroyed in the Civil War. Kingston Lacy has been renovated and houses a renowned collection of paintings.

5 Cranborne
Cranbourne Chase is part of the UK's sixth largest Area of Oustanding Natural Beauty and is characterised by gently rolling chalk slopes.

6 Poole
Poole's large natural harbour determined its future as a port, and made it an important centre for boat and yacht building. Poole quay is usually busy with visitors and locals, whereas the old part of the harbour is much quieter.

BOURNEMOUTH MAP REF SZ0991

Bournemouth is the queen of the south coast holiday resorts, with its 6 miles (9.6km) of fine golden sands, its pier complete with striped deck chairs and theatre for nostalgic summer shows, its orderly winter gardens, its palm-tree lined parks and compact town centre dedicated to serious shopping, as well as a vast hinterland of suburban sprawl.

Unlike its more serious neighbour, Poole, Bournemouth has never really been anything other than a resort. It was a small village in the early 19th century, at the time when many of the pine trees that now scent the air were first planted. Blessed with a mild climate, and a south-facing location in a sheltered cleft, the settlement boomed towards the end of the 19th century, and most of the town's central buildings date from this period, with Victorian buildings interspersed with some later art deco. New luxury blocks of offices and modern accommodation may have changed the skyline for ever, but the towns heart has a comfortable, old-fashioned feel that still appeals to many holiday-makers.

The town centre is shaped around the Lower, Centre and Upper Gardens, a long, leafy park around the flowing Bourne stream, with magnificent island flowerbeds, scenic tethered balloon flights, an aviary, a mini-golf centre and various refreshment stops. Around the upper end and the Square cluster all the main shopping streets, with arcades leading off the largely pedestrianised Old Christchurch Road. The most appealing of these is the glazed 1866 Victorian Arcade housing well-known Dingles department store and designer outlets including Gucci and Karen Millen. Beales is Bournemouth's large independent department store. Opposite it is St Peter's Church, with Arts and Crafts wall paintings, a chapel dedicated to the Oxford Movement reformer John Keble, and the grave of novelist Mary Shelley (and the heart of her brother, the Romantic poet) in the churchyard.

The lower end of the park runs past the Pavilion Theatre, under the main road and out onto the seafront, with the pier just ahead. Bournemouth's pier is a functional affair, reinforced with ugly concrete that has seen it survive when others along this coastline have been washed away. Photographs at the far end show how it was partly demolished during World War II to prevent its use in a possible German invasion. Now it has a pier theatre and amusements, and great views back to the town, and the western beaches with their beach huts tucked under the sandy cliffs. A land train offers transport up and down the seafront. The twin domes near the pier entrance mark the aquarium, and the modern glazed building on the seafront

■ Insight

BEACH HUTS

These wooden chalets are an integral feature of seaside resorts, and date back to the days when sea-bathers were taken modestly out into the shallows in horse-drawn wooden huts on wheels, before entering the water in full costume. Today they offer a bit of home on the beach, and sell for tens of thousands of pounds. At Bournemouth, however, you can rent them by the day – ask at the tourist office.

is the IMAX cinema complex. Set behind this, on the East Cliff, you will find the interestingly turreted Russell-Cotes Art Gallery and Museum, which is home to a collection of fine Victorian paintings and treasures from around the world.

BOVINGTON MAP REF SY8388

The Royal Artillery, the Infantry and the Royal Armoured Corps train their drivers on a £6 million all-weather circuit near Bovington, and there has been military training in the area since the first tanks were introduced during World War I. Bovington's Tank Museum explains it all, and has the world's largest collection of around 250 armoured fighting vehicles, and exhibits from 25 countries – you don't even have to be a tank fanatic to thoroughly enjoy it. Mock battles and rides are offered in summer. One corner is devoted to 'Lawrence of Arabia', who has strong links to this part of Dorset.

In nearby Moreton churchyard is a stark slab of white marble inscribed: 'To the dear memory of T E Lawrence, Fellow of All Souls College, Oxford. Born 16 August 1888, died 19 May 1935.'

The brilliant, enigmatic and haunted figure of Lawrence continues to intrigue people. As British liaison officer to the Arab Revolt, Lawrence proved himself a leader with an ambitious personality and an extensive knowledge of strategic warfare. His flamboyant courage and adoption of Arabic dress gave him heroic status as Akaba was captured in 1917, and Damascus achieved in the following year. Lawrence remained involved in Arab affairs even after the war, lobbying unsuccessfully for Arab independence.

■ Visit

MORETON GLASS

Moreton church was rebuilt after bomb damage in 1940, and its chief delight is its windows. What from outside looks like plain glass, from inside the glass is revealed to be engraved with a vivid flow of delicate pictorial designs. The etching is the work of the late Lawrence Whistler (more of his work can be seen in Salisbury Cathedral). The window (1982) in the Trinity Chapel particularly rewards closer inspection; it is an anonymous memorial to an airman killed over France during the war, and tells of a brief marriage cut short, illustrated by magnolia blossoms, a sunburst, and a crashed biplane.

Finding fame a millstone, he joined the ranks of the RAF in 1922, seeking a degree of security and regular life as Aircraftsman Ross.

Discovered, he first enlisted in the Tank Corps at Bovington in 1923 as Private T E Shaw, and moved to Dorset, buying a derelict house at nearby Clouds Hill (now National Trust) as an evening and weekend retreat. Clouds Hill is a bachelor house, with a gramophone, well stocked book shelves, comfortable firesides and few frills; it became his 'earthly paradise'. Lawrence finished writing his account of the Arab Revolt, *The Seven Pillars of Wisdom* (1926), here, and in 1925 rejoined the RAF.

In 1935 he retired to Clouds Hill, but on 13 May that year, returning home on his Brough Superior SS-100, he swerved to avoid cyclists and was thrown from the motorbike. He died five days later; the legend is still very much alive.

Corfe Castle Circuit

A loop to Kingston from the romantic ruins of Corfe Castle. The route takes in Corfe Common and part of the Purbeck Way incorporating downland, heath and village streets. The Common is crisscrossed by narrow bridlepaths and walkways, and after completing this walk, you might like to return to explore different routes. The National Trust also offers guided walks here.

Route Directions

1 From the car park bear right then right again on to West Street. At the end, go straight on over a cattle grid. Bear left on a path across the heath; the line to guide you is Kingston church tower. Cross duckboards and go uphill, forking right by a tumulus, and then walk to the right of a stone block. Continue over the brow of the hill and then descend, keeping in line with the church tower. The path gradually veers right and it leaves the Common by way of a kissing gate, stiles and footbridges.

2 Bear half-left across a field, and across the next, regaining the line of the tower. Go over a bridge and ascend a wooded path. Climb over a stile and continue up the left edge of a field. Maintain your direction after you cross the next stile. Go through a thick hedge and head straight across the next field (the flag pole on the church tower being the line) to a kissing gate and turn right up a track. On the ascent fork left, taking the path up through the woods.

3 At the top, turn left to the road and walk down through the village. At the junction by the Scott Arms turn right. After the converted church,

go over a stile on the left and bear half-right, signposted to Afflington. Pass through a gate at the bottom corner of the field and continue along the left boundary of the next field to a stile in the corner. Shortly after, bear left down through scrubland, then turn left on to a stony track. As the track bears right take the path left (Purbeck Way) over a stile and go down the track left into a field.

4 Turn right, go through a gate and soon go right over a stile. Cross a narrow wooded strip to a stile and turn left beside the woods. Climb over a further stile and proceed straight on, soon to bear left through a gate and around the left edge of a field. Turn left over another stile and over a footbridge, then continue over a further stile and turn sharp right. Cross a metalled drive, a stile, a causeway and then a bridge on to the Common.

5 Go straight on over Corfe Common towards the castle ruins. Bear left at a concrete marker, and proceed right to a gate. Cross the B3069, go through a gate and straight on, later bearing right behind houses. Go through a kissing gate and follow the path (still signed Purbeck Way) towards

Route facts

DISTANCE/TIME 4.25 miles (6.8 km) 2h

MAP OS OS Explorer OL 15 Purbeck & South Dorset

START Corfe Castle; village car park (fee), grid ref: SY 958818

TRACKS Village lanes, rocky lanes (slippery after rain), moorland tracks, grassy paths

GETTING TO THE START
The small township of Corfe Castle stands on the A351, midway between Wareham and Swanage, 5 miles (8km) southeast of Wareham. The car park is off West Street, close to the village centre.

THE PUB The Greyhound Inn, The Square, Corfe Castle. Tel: 01929 480205

❶ The main A351 through Corfe is often busy and dangerous.

the centre of Corfe. After it winds through some housing walk across fields leading into a playground. Turn left and then right into West Street to reach the square.

6 Turn left by the castle on the path below the walls. Go left up the road and soon left again by a gate and over a stile (by a sign to The Rings). Cross the fields via a series of gates to return to the car park in West Street.

CORFE CASTLE MAP REF SY9682

Corfe is the best-known village on the so-called Isle of Purbeck, and is packed with pubs, tea rooms and little shops that make it a magnet for summer visitors, who are rewarded with excellent walking in the area.

The huge and toothy ruin of Corfe Castle seems to fill the gap in the wall of the Purbeck Hills with its presence. It has a grim history. In AD 978 a youthful King Edward (the Martyr) was murdered here by his stepmother; his body was buried without ceremony at Wareham, while his half-brother took the throne as Ethelred II (the Unready). However, stories of miracles soon resulted in the exhumation of Edward's body. It was transported to Shaftesbury, where an abbey grew up in his honour.

Around 1106 the big square Norman keep was built, to defend against raiders from the sea and to impress the local populace. King John used it as a lifelong prison for his niece Eleanor, a potential threat to his throne. Edward II, deposed by his wife, was imprisoned here briefly.

During the Civil War the castle's owner, Sir John Bankes, eventually sided with the King, leaving his spirited wife Mary, with a handful of women and just five men, to fight off a siege in 1642. History books state that the 500-strong Parliamentarian army stripped all the lead from the church roof to make their bullets, and stored their gunpowder and shot in the organ pipes, but they failed to take the castle. After a second siege, the castle was betrayed in 1646 by one of its defenders, and after it was abandoned it was destroyed to prevent its use again.

South of Corfe, Worth Matravers is a picturesque village of lichen-encrusted grey cottages, complete with duck pond. Men from here have worked in the local quarries for centuries, and Purbeck marble (in fact a type of limestone) from this area was famously sent inland for the building of Salisbury Cathedral. The Square & Compass, an old fashioned pub with smoked beams and a big stone hearth, is a favourite with walkers. On the nearby cliffs stands 800-year-old St Adhelm's Chapel, a sturdy, buttressed brown cube, that has only one tiny little window. Near the coastguard station is a steel memorial to the brilliant work of radar developers here in 1940–42.

CRANBORNE CHASE
MAP REF ST9317

Cranborne Chase covers an area of around 100sq miles (260sq km) of the long chalk massif which straddles the Dorset–Wiltshire border to the east of Shaftesbury. It was once a popular royal hunting preserve, but is now mostly rolling grassland with pockets of mixed woodland. On the northwestern flanks, Fontmell and Melbury Downs are particularly beautiful, and covered with butterflies in summer. To the southeast lie a string of attractive little villages, including Tarrants Gunville and Hinton, and Chettle. Sixpenny Handley has one of the oddest names in England – which alone justifies a visit – but if you go there expecting a romantic 1950s throwback, be prepared for a surprise. Much of the old village was destroyed by fire in 1892; today it is a bold, lively modern village with lots of new housing.

■ Visit

SMEDMORE HOUSE

The Clavell family have been at Smedmore since the 13th century, and Smedmore House, a handsome twin-bayed affair dating from 1761, keeps a firm eye on activities in the bay still. It is occasionally open in high summer when its attractive gardens are in bloom. The Clavell Tower folly, now dangerously close to the crumbling cliff edge, is currently the subject of a major rescue project.

Compared with other parts of Dorset, there are few settlements here, a sign of the feudal state in which the land was held until 1830. After the last Ice Age, Dorset was smothered in a growth of broadleaved woodland, including species such as oak, ash and elm, known as 'native'. As the human population grew and spread, this woodland was gradually cleared for its timber and to make way for agricultural land. The hunting 'forest' of Cranborne Chase claimed by William the Conqueror therefore included open sections of heath, downland, scrub and rough pasture, as well as patches of remaining woodland.

Little of the original forest remains on the Chase – most woods show signs of mixed planting and many generations of coppicing, which was designed to produce a continuous supply of timber for everyday use. The effects of planting for timber in the later 18th century can be seen in the widespread stands of non-native beech across the Chase. Trees for timber were planted compactly to encourage tall, straight growth with a minimum of interruption from side branches. The pursuit of fallow deer on the Chase provided the mainstay of royal sport, and they can still be seen here, most visible in the early evening.

In the early 18th century, the hunting rights on Cranbourne Chase passed to the powerful Pitt-Rivers family, who proceeded to rule the area like a feudal manor. Operating under the so-called Chase Law it became a byway for many smugglers and a refuge for criminals. In 1830, after much local campaigning, Chase Law was abandoned.

KIMMERIDGE BAY

MAP REF SY9189

There's a bleakness about Kimmeridge Bay which the energy of the youthful windsurfers riding the waves and the cheerful picture of families pottering in the rock pools can't quite dispel. Giant slabs of black rock shelving out to sea, with crumbling cliffs topped by clumps of wild cabbage, create something of this mood, and the slow, steady nodding donkey-head of the oil well above a terrace of unmistakably industrial cottages reinforces it.

Iron Age tribes first spotted the potential of the band of bituminous shale that runs through Kimmeridge, polishing it up into different blackstone ornaments, and even chair and table legs. The shale, permeated with crude oil, is also known as Kimmeridge coal, but many attempts to work it on an industrial scale failed, including alum extraction (for dyeing) in the 16th century, and using the coal to fuel a glassworks in the 17th century. The shale was worked in the 19th century, and for one brief period the street lights of Paris were lit by gas extracted from the shale oil, but nothing lasted for very long. Since 1959 British Petroleum has drilled 1,716 feet (520m) below the sea; its beam engine sucks out some 80 barrels of crude oil a day. Transported to the Wytch Farm collection point, near Corfe, the oil is then pumped to Hamble, ready to be shipped around the world

Its combination of clear, shallow water, double low tides and accessible rocky ledges make Kimmeridge an ideal choice for an underwater nature reserve. The double low tide is at its best in the afternoons – effectively, the water may stay low all afternoon, allowing optimum access to the fingers of rock that stretch out into the bay, revealing an amazing world of rock pools and gullies alive with seaweeds, anemones and creatures that include crabs, blennies and the more bizarre pipe-fish. Learn more at the Fine Foundation Marine Centre. Kimmeridge is part of the Smedmore estate, and accessed via a private toll road.

In contrast to Kimmeridge, Tyneham, over the hill, is a cosy farming village clustered around its church in a glorious valley. As you get up close, however, you realise that it's impossibly neat, like an idealised film set. Inside the church is an exhibition to explain all: the villagers were asked to give up their homes in December 1943 for the 'war effort', and Tyneham became absorbed into the vast acreage of the Lulworth Ranges, part of the live firing range. It is a touching memorial, though perhaps nothing can make up for the fact that the villagers were never allowed back to their homes.

KINGSTON LACY MAP REF ST9802

Kingston Lacy is an elegant mansion dating from 1663 and is set in extensive parkland northwest of Wimborne. The house, which has a particularly fine collection of paintings, was built for the Bankes family after the destruction of Corfe Castle in the Civil War, and the house was then remodelled in the 19th century by Sir Charles Barry. One of the most unusual chambers is the Spanish Room, with its walls adorned with gilded leather. On the 8,000-acre (3,240ha) estate, Conegar Capers is a woodland play area for younger children, and there are lots of good waymarked walks.

One of the most obvious legacies of the Roman invasion of Britain in AD 43 is the network of straight military roads that they constructed across the country. Four of the most important Roman routes met at the hub of Badbury Rings, just north of Kingston Lacy. The most famous and visible of these is Ackling Dyke, the major road which linked London (*Londinium*) with Old Sarum (*Sorviodunum*), Dorchester (*Durnovaria*, the *civitas* or Roman capital of the Dorset area) and Exeter (*Iscarduniorum*).

Badbury Rings was a massive hill-fort occupying a spectacular vantage point. Bronze Age burial barrows in the area confirm a settlement in around 2000 BC, and the rings and ditches date from the 6th century BC, when Dorset was inhabited by the Durotriges tribe. It is a peaceful spot, softened by the trees on top, a recent replanting to replicate what was there in 1761. The hill fort is approached via a magnificent avenue of beeches planted by William Bankes.

LULWORTH COVE

MAP REF SY8380

Lulworth Cove is an almost perfectly circular bay in the rolling line of limestone cliffs that form Dorset's southern coast. It provides a safe anchorage for small fishing boats and pleasure craft, and a sun-trap of safe water for summer bathers. The wave-polished grey, black and red pebbles of the shingle beach, from wren's egg to ostrich egg in size, are reminiscent of childhood jars of pebble sweets. To the west, along the South West Coast Path, lie rolling, chalky downs and the landmark of Durdle Door, below the cliffs. To the east lie Worbarrow and Mupe bays.

The geology of the area is intriguing, and a visit to the Heritage Centre in the village will help you to identify the various rock formations. The oldest layer is the gleaming white Portland stone, much employed by Christopher Wren in his rebuilding of London. It is a fine-grained oolite around 140 million years old, consisting of tightly compressed fossilised shells, and occasionally throws up giant flat-coiled ammonites, called a titanite, which may be seen incorporated decoratively into many house walls across Purbeck. Above this is a thick layer of Purbeck marble, a rich limestone where dinosaur, reptile and fish fossils are usually found. The soft layer above this consists of Wealden beds – a belt of colourful sedimentary clays, silts and sands that are unstable and prone to landslips when exposed. Crumbly white chalk overlays this, the remains of microscopic sea creatures and shells deposited over a long period of time when a deep sea covered much of Dorset, some 75 million years ago.

The Fossil Forest in the sea cliffs east of Lulworth Cove is an intriguing oddity, but don't go looking for stone trees. What you see are the stone rings where sediment has bubbled up around tree-trunks that rotted away millions of years ago. Together with the fossilised soil discovered beneath the tree boles, they give an insight into Jurassic life here, 135 million years ago.

Lulworth Castle Park at nearby East Lulworth was a hunting lodge, built four-square in 1608 with pepperpot towers. Gutted by fire in 1929, it is now a handsome shell, and still only partly restored. Other attractions on the estate include a circular chapel, an animal farm and an adventure playground for children, and summer jousting events.

Nearly 200 rescued and endangered apes and monkeys have found a new, welcoming home at Monkey World, a few miles north of Wool. The park has of 65 acres (26ha) of woodland, where the monkeys can recuperate in a safe environment made specifically for them.

■ Insight

THE DOLLS HOUSE

As yopu make your way down to the pretty harbour in Lulworth, look out for the tiny baby-blue painted timber Dolls House. It is a restored Victorian fisherman's cottage dating from 1861, now a fishing museum, and you may find it difficult to believe that 11 children were raised in this tiny house. Contrast its cramped simplicity with the cottage orné opposite, complete with big diamond-pane windows and a cosy thatched roof.

MILTON ABBAS MAP REF ST8102

It is the natural order of villages to grow over generations, to spread out a little, to develop secret corners, and to reflect different ages, abilities and tastes in its buildings. Rarely do you find a village quite so symmetrical as Milton Abbas, whose regular whitewashed houses, identical in design, are placed neatly on either side of a narrow defile, thatched cowl opposite thatched cowl. It's an unnatural and slightly eerie sight. On closer inspection, you see that rebels have managed to sneak on a porch here, a coat of cream-coloured paint there, but nothing to seriously spoil the effect of planned perfection. There appear to have been no concessions either on houses that were once a bakery and a forge, although the tailor's house had bow windows for extra light.

The answer lies with the great house round the corner, the dream of Joseph and Caroline Damer, who bought Milton Abbey in 1752. It was on a fabulous site, but the house left much to be desired. In 1771 they decided to build something grander, to include a landscaped park by 'Capability' Brown. But the ugly and untidy township around the abbey was spoiling the view, and would have to go.

And so a new hamlet of thatched cottages was built out of sight in a narrow valley, and the villagers were moved, whether they liked it or not. The houses look generous, but in fact each little block was two independent family dwellings, separated by a shared central hall. What the villagers had to say about the near-vertical valley walls behind their shiny new homes is not recorded, but some steep terraced gardens were eventually dug out, and are one of the attractive features of Milton Abbas today.

The Damers are buried in splendour in the abbey church; their house, never the architectural success they had hoped for, became a school in 1954.

Nearby Winterborne Clenston is altogether more organic, combining a pretty Victorian rectory with a magnificent Tudor manor house and a medieval tithe barn with a steep chequerboard roof of alternating red and black squares. The Gothic church of St Nicholas, dating from 1840, is a perfectly proportioned miniature.

POOLE MAP REF SZ0291

Unlike its frivolous and glitzy neighbour Bournemouth, Poole has an ancient and serious heart that gives it a different character. It grew up in the Middle Ages as the main port on one of the world's greatest and safest natural harbours, taking over in maritime importance from Wareham. Today it is still very much a working port, with marinas packed out with expensive sailing yachts, a small surviving fishing fleet, many productive boatyards creating some of the costliest and sleekest luxury motorboats made in the world, and cross-Channel ferries – the biggest craft to negotiate the narrow entrance to the harbour at Sandbanks.

The best place to start an exploration of Old Poole is the Quay – the attractive old waterfront, with views across the harbour and more immediately, to the boatyards. The Cockle Trail is a walking trail around the historic town – pick up a leaflet at the tourist office.

At the western end the Quay is lined with stylish old buildings, including the brick Customs House of 1813, as well as the pillared Coastguard office of 1820, all on an appealingly small scale. There are old pubs along here too, including the Poole Arms with is green-glazed tile frontage, and the handsome King's Head, set slightly back at the lower end of the High Street. This is Poole's main shopping street, lined with small and largely practical shops – for bigger high-street names head inland to the modern Dolphin Shopping Centre. As you stroll eastwards along the Quay, past the town marina with its gleaming moored yachts, you soon reach the rustier hulks of the fishing fleet. There is a small museum in a wooden shed to explore, its paint faded and peeling – it is the home of the old Thomas Kirk Wright lifeboat, which took part as one of the flotilla of 'Little Ships' in the brave evacuation of Allied soldiers from Dunkirk in May, 1940.

Between the Quay and the end tip of the sheltering sandspit of Sandbanks, the coastline seems like one long haven or park dedicated to varied watersports and sailing. Paragliding, wakeboarding and kitesurfing are favourite activities in these shallow, sheltered waters.

Laid inland from Sandbanks amid elegant and spacious Edwardian villas, Compton Acres is a huge, privately owned pleasure garden established in the 1920s. As well as themed gardens which include a Wooded Valley, a pretty Grotto, a Water Garden and Roman and Japanese gardens, the 10-acre (4ha) site also has two restaurants for fine dining, a delicatessen and craft and gift shops.

The famous Poole Pottery is 4 miles (6.5km) from the Old Town, and offers factory tours, or pop into the factory outlet on the Quay, where you can also paint your own plate or bowl.

STUDLAND MAP REF SZ0383

The glorious sands in Studland Bay are justly famous, and attract over a million visitors a year, so it's worth getting up early to have them to yourself. You are unlikely to be alone for long, though. As you progress up the beach, getting warmer, you can shed your clothes with impunity, for the upper stretch opens its arms to naturists – and even on a bright winter's morning you'll spot brave souls sunbathing naked in the shelter of the marram-covered dunes. Off shore, big, sleek motor boats let rip as they emerge from the constraints of Poole Harbour. Watch out, too, for the orange and blue of the Poole lifeboat on manoeuvres, and the yellow and black pilot boat nipping out to lead in the tankers. Jet-skiers zip around the more sedate sailing yachts, all dodging the small fishing boats. It's a perfect seaside harmony, complete with wheedling, soaring gulls.

Behind the beach lies the old rugged heath, part of the same nature reserve that is in the care of English Nature and the National Trust. They are currently working together on a programme of restoration, reclaiming heath that had become farmland, and clearing scrub and maintaining controlled grazing to prevent it all reverting to woodland. All six of Britain's reptiles – common lizard, sand lizard, smooth snake, adder, grass snake, slow worm – live on the heath.

STUDLAND

Durdle Door and Lulworth Cove

An exhilarating walk on a stunning stretch of coastline visiting Durdle Door, a spectacular natural rock arch in the sea, and Lulworth Cove before turning inland and skirting the village of West Lulworth. The white chalk that breaks through the soil here underlies Dorset's famous downland and is seen in the exposed soft, eroded cliffs at White Nothe.

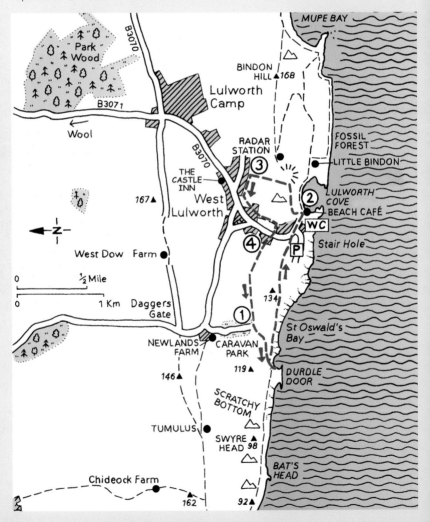

Route Directions

1 From the corner of the car park at Durdle Door Caravan Park take the path down to Durdle Door. Return the same way but before steeply ascending fork right, signed to Lulworth Cove. Follow the path along the coast and down to the cove (the Heritage Centre and Stair Hole are worth visiting).

2 Turn sharp left up steps, signed to Bindon Hill. Walk through a wooded area to a stile, then turn sharp right to skirt the rim of the cove. Near the top take the path left to Bindon Hill and on the brow, at a junction with a wider path, turn right. Walk across ancient earthworks and by the entrance to Lulworth Army Ranges, then turn left down towards the village of West Lulworth. Cross a stile and bear half-left across a field, crossing the stile on the left just before the bottom.

3 Continue along a fenced path at the back of the village. The path swings left up some steps (steps right lead down to the Main Street where you turn right for the Castle Inn), then along to an unmade road. At the junction with Bindon Road turn left, and in 25yds (23m) turn right over a stile, signed to Lulworth Cove.

In 10yds (9m) fork right through a gate and keep to the right edge of the field. At the waymarker, turn right over a stile, signed Durdle Door. Descend the fenced path to the road.

4 Turn right, and in 50yds (46m) turn left to Durdle Door. Cross the stile and walk along the left-hand edge of a field. After the next stile ascend some steps through a small wood to a stile and turn right along a chalk path, signed to Durdle Door Camp Site. Ignore the parallel track, and continue across fields. After four stiles return to the corner of the car park.

Route facts

DISTANCE/TIME 3.25 miles (5.3km) 2h

MAP OS Explorer OL 15 Purbeck & South Dorset

START Car park (fee) above Durdle Door, grid ref: SY 811804

TRACKS Stone path, grassy tracks, tarmac, stiles

GETTING TO THE START
From the A352 west of Wareham take the B3070 south for East Lulworth and continue to West Lulworth. Pass the Castle Inn and turn first right, passing the church. In 0.75 mile (1.2km) turn left, past the Durdle Door Caravan Park, to the car park.

THE PUB The Castle Inn, West Lulworth.
Tel: 01929 400311;
www.thecastleinn-lulworth cove.co.uk

❶ Take heed of warning signs – steep paths (up and down) and cliff edges. A short walk but really for fitter, older children.

Poole & the Isle of Purbeck

The Isle of Purbeck is the fascinating area to the west of Poole, a landlocked island of high hills and sea cliffs. The route entails a complete circuit of Poole Harbour, with a short ferry ride at the end. On the way you will see lovely villages and a deserted village, sheltered bays, a ruined castle, seaside resorts, a seaside pier and the long sandy beach of Studland.

Route Directions

Explore the quayside at Poole. with its shops, pubs and the Poole pottery factory outlet.

1 Leave Poole town centre and follow the signs for Hamworthy and Poole Bridge. Cross the bridge, by the Sunseeker boatyard, and continue towards Hamworthy and Rockley Park. After 2.5 miles (4km) pass under two railway bridges, with Upton Park signed to your left. Continue through Upton, and at the double roundabout by the clock tower turn left, signed Lytchett Minster. Pass through Lytchett Minster. At the roundabout with the A35, go straight ahead, signed A351 Wareham. Continue ahead across several roundabouts and through traffic lights, following signs to Wareham. Go straight on at the next roundabout, signed Corfe Castle, and bear left at the next roundabout, and follow signs for Wareham.

Stop in Wareham to explore this historic town on the banks of the River Frome.

2 In Wareham continue down the high street, then cross the river. Continue to Stoborough and bear right, signed Creech. At the junction with the A351 turn left and immediately right, signed Creech, Steeple and Kimmeridge. Turn right onto a minor road, signed to East and West Lulworth.

The route passes through an area of farmland and open heath that is typical of the area, with pine forests, and parkland at East Holme. There is a stunning view of the long chalk ridge of the Purbeck Hills off to your left.

3 After 2.5 miles (4km), turn left for East Lulworth – look out for tanks crossing, this is all part of the Lulworth army training area. Continue through the village of East Lulworth. At the T-junction turn left and continue on through West Lulworth village to Lulworth Cove.

Park on the right, by the heritage centre, to explore the cove and coastal path.

4 Retrace your route for 3 miles (5km) back up the hill and almost to the gates of Lulworth Castle. Turn right here, and take the next narrow turning right, signed Tyneham Village.

This winding road rises along the back of the ridge and up to the crest, with superb views across the country inland.

5 After 4.5 miles (7km), Whiteways Viewpoint is on your right.

Enjoy views down over the coast and Kimmeridge Bay, and to Poole Harbour straight ahead of you.

6 Continue, and a turning circle on the left marks the tight right turn down to Tyneham village. Follow the road down to the church.

Explore the deserted village which was evacuated in 1943.

7 Return up the road to the turning circle and turn right. Just before another viewpoint turn right towards Steeple and Kimmeridge. The narrow road descends sharply. Turn right, signed to Kimmeridge and the sea. The road crosses a valley and goes up a ridge before descending to pass by Smedmore House. Finally, it zig-zags down through Kimmeridge village. Note: a toll is payable if you want to continue down to the beach car park on Kimmeridge Bay. The pebble beach here, with its long rock ledges and numerous rock pools, is popular with families and water sports enthusiasts.

8 Retrace your route back across the valley and turn right, signed to Church Knowle and Corfe Castle. After 1.5 miles (2.5km) pass through Church Knowle. Continue towards Corfe, circling the base of the castle mound, and turn right to Swanage on the A351. Make your way through the centre of Corfe village. On the other side of the village turn right, signed to Langton Matravers. Cross the Common. Follow the road left, and soon turn right, which is signed Worth Matravers. Continue for a mile (1.6km), passing the quarry on your right. Park your car in the car park just above Worth Matravers. Walk down the hill and bear right to visit the duck pond and the church of St Nicholas.

9 Turn left at the Square and Compass pub, at the sign to Langton Matravers. Turn right at the main road and descend to Langton Matravers. At the junction with the A351 turn right and then follow signs for Swanage town centre and to the beach.
The traditional seaside resort of Swanage has a gently shelving sandy beach and a Victorian pier.

10 Leave Swanage on the coast road, signed Studland, Poole and Bournemouth via toll ferry. After 3 miles (5km) turn right for Studland on the B3351. Continue to the ferry crossing Studland Heath. The toll ferry crossing to Sandbanks takes about 10 minutes only, but expect to queue in high season. Follow the B3369 coast road, past Compton Acres, back into the centre of Poole.

PUNCH & JUDY
SWANAGE
SHOWS DAILY
12.30 2.30 4.00

Adults & Children
£1.00

SWANAGE MAP REF SZ0378

In the early 19th century Swanage was a small, bustling industrial port shipping stone from the 60 or more quarries in the area. A growing fashion for sea-bathing would in time change the focus of the town for ever. The real changes to the face of Swanage came, however, with the extraordinary collecting habit of one George Burt, a contractor with an eye for ornate architecture.

With his uncle John Mowlem, a local stonemason and philanthropist, Burt shipped marble from the old quarries of Purbeck up to London, where many old buildings were being knocked down to make way for new construction. He was reluctant to see such fine stonework discarded, so Burt salvaged large whole pieces, transported them back to Dorset as ballast, and re-erected them in his home town, giving Swanage an 'instant' architectural heritage.

The Town Hall is a prime example of Burt's influence. He had donated a reasonably plain and simple building to the town in 1872; but in 1883 he added a façade by Wren, which he had rescued from the Mercers' Hall in London's Cheapside. In a park near the pier you can see a grand archway removed from Hyde Park Corner, and three statues and some columns rescued from Billingsgate Market. There is also an absurd but rather elegant clock tower, removed from the south end of London Bridge in 1867, where it had been set as a memorial to the Duke of Wellington.

Durleston Castle is an original folly by Burt dating from 1887, designed from the start as a clifftop restaurant on Durleston Head. Facts and figures from around the world are carved into great stone slabs set into the walls below. Burt added a large, segmented stone globe of the world. It is grey and rather disappointing, but nevertheless in a beautiful spot where you can sit during the evening, watching the sunset fade the sea into the sky, with the lighthouse at the end of the Needles winking from across the water.

At Studland Museum and Heritage Centre you can learn more about the area, including tales of smuggling and the development of Purbeck's stone quarrying industry. And for a nominal fee, try the delights of Swanage's Victorian pier, which announces penny-in-the-slot machines and 'Wot the butler saw' – no seaside visit can be complete without it. The pier suffered in the past from neglect and threat of demolition, but is now undergoing restoration.

TOLPUDDLE MAP REF SY7995

Tolpuddle is a peaceful village tucked in the fold of a hill beside the A35. It is associated with a political revolt in the 19th century, celebrated with the Martyrs' Museum, commemorated in the name of the local pub, and marked at various other points.

The Martyrs' Tree stands on the little green at the heart of Tolpuddle. It was a meeting point for the Friendly Society of Agricultural Labourers, a group formed to peaceably lobby their masters for much better pay, at a time when a local labourer's wage was just seven shillings a week – around three shillings below what was paid elsewhere in Dorset, and barely enough to feed a family on. Such unions were unlawful, and George and James Loveless, Thomas and John Standfield, James Brine and James Hammett were picked out as ringleaders and troublemakers, and convicted at Dorchester in 1834.

The six men were duly exiled, but their case was unusual. Despite their conviction for 'administering unlawful oaths', their seven-year sentences were quashed after public outrage, and the Tolpuddle Martyrs were pardoned. The processes of law and communication were slow in those times, and it was five years before they all returned home.

George Loveless, a well-spoken Methodist lay preacher whose statue sits outside the museum, had developed a taste for life beyond these valleys, and after his return he emigrated to Canada with four of the others. James Hammet was the only one to die in the village, and his grave is in the local churchyard.

Between 1800 and 1850 some 1,800 individuals convicted of political crimes were shipped out to Australia, effectively silencing dangerous elements.

Athelhampton, one of England's most majestic old mansions, is just down the road to the west, and well worth a visit. Parts of it date from 1485, and the house is stuffed with treasures, from Tudor architecture in the Great Hall to a carved Charles I tester bed. Allow time to explore the world-famous gardens with their yew topiary and fountains.

WAREHAM MAP REF SY9387

Wareham bills itself as a Saxon walled town, but a great fire in 1762 destroyed many of the older buildings, and what you see today in the centre is mainly Georgian. The town has had a chequered history, its status as the major trading port on Poole Harbour making it quite vulnerable to attacks from marauding Vikings, and then undermined when the River Frome silted up badly during the Middle Ages.

One survivor from the town's earliest heyday is St Martin's Church. Dating from around 1030, it's the oldest church in Dorset, and stands on the northern section of the ancient town walls. It has some remarkable fragments of 12th-century frescoes, and now houses an effigy of T E Lawrence, by sculptor Eric Kennington, in Arab costume and with his head resting on a camel saddle. Learn more about Lawrence of Arabia in the redbrick Town Museum on the High Street. This broad and gracious street is the main thoroughfare of the town, leading down to the river, and is lined with interesting shops and eating places.

Stroll along the quiet heath road through Ridge, once a busy river port in its own right, to the hamlet of Arne, 3 miles (4.8km) away near the shores of Poole Harbour. Many of the houses here

■ Insight

T E LAWRENCE

The sculptured effigy of Lawrence was made between 1936 and 1939 by Eric Kennington, the official war artist, and was intended as a memorial for St Paul's Cathedral. However, on Lawrence's death St Paul's, then Westminster Abbey and finally Salisbury Cathedral all turned it down, and the ancient church at Wareham became its less glamourous home.

were demolished during World War II when the army used the village as a training ground, and what's left remains in sleepy retirement. There is a 13th-century church to explore, and a nature reserve where rare Dartford warblers breed and nightjars sing.

North of Wareham, at Sandford, is Farmer Palmer's, a great family farm park, complete with hands-on animal feeding, milking cows, tractor rides and amusements – perfect for the under-8s.

WIMBORNE MINSTER

MAP REF SU0200

This attractive old market town on the River Stour made its fortunes in ancient times on the profits of wool. Its most distinctive feature is the Minster Church of St Cuthberga, whose squat, square towers dominate the town centre. Its foundation dates back to AD 705, though the present building dates from some 400 years later. One of the town's most fascinating elements is the library, which was founded in 1686 for the free use of the townspeople, and consisting of 350 (mainly theological) volumes. To prevent the theft of these items, the books were chained to the shelves – workhouse orphans made the chains. The Quarter Jack clock on the west tower is a much-loved local icon, with its brightly painted soldier striking the quarter hours with a hammer.

The nearby village Cornmarket, is a sheltered square, with an old pub, the White Hart, that becomes the centre of activities around the Folk Festival. The King's Head Hotel on the old main Square was formerly a coaching inn.

■ Insight

THE RIVER STOUR

The Stour supports a rich variety of wildlife. Most obvious are the birds, with mallards and mute swans on the water, moorhens, warblers and buntings in the tall reed beds, and grey herons and exotic white egrets fishing in the shallows. Trout, roach, perch, dace, minnows and eels live in the water, and in summer look out for orange tip, peacock and clouded yellow butterflies, dragonflies and damselflies.

The Priest's House Museum on the High Street is a medieval house with some later additions, originally built for use by the priests at the Minster but was later occupied by a succession of different tradespeople, including an ironmonger, a tobacconist and a printer. It is full of the domestic paraphernalia of years gone by, including a Victorian kitchen and a tinsmith's workshop. The walled garden, which leads gently down to the river, is a particular delight.

Wimborne has its own model town, carefully created to 1/10 scale some 50 years ago, which is the primary focus for children's activities such as a putting lawn, and special events for all ages throughout the year.

East of Wimborne, at Hampreston, lie Knoll Gardens, a superb modern garden and specialist nursery displaying grasses, perennials and much more. To the northeast lies Stapehill, the site of a 19th-century abbey now transformed into extensive, beautiful formal as well as informal gardens, with a countryside museum and farmyard. There are also resident craftspeople.

TOURIST INFORMATION CENTRES

Bournemouth
Westover Road.
Tel: 0845 051 1700;
www.bournemouth.co.uk

Poole
Enefco House, Poole Quay.
Tel: 01202 253253;
www.pooletourism.com

Swanage
The White House,
Shore Road.
Tel: 01929 422885;
www.swanage.gov.uk

Wareham
Holy Trinity Church,
South Street.
Tel: 01929 522740;
www.purbeck.gov.uk

Wimborne
29 High Street.
Tel: 01202 886116;
www.ruraldorset.com

PLACES OF INTEREST

Arne RSPB Reserve
Wareham.
Tel: 01929 553360

Athelhampton House & Gardens
Tel: 01305 848363;
www.athelhampton.co.uk

Bournemouth Aviation Museum
Bournemouth Airport.
Tel: 01202 580858;
www.aviation-museum.co.uk

Bovington Tank Museum
Tel: 01929 405096;
www.tankmuseum.org

Brownsea Island (NT)
Offshore Poole Harbour.
Tel: 01202 707744

Clouds Hill (NT)
Near Bovington.
Tel: 01929 405616

Compton Acres
Tel: 01202 700778;
www.comptonacres.co.uk

Corfe Castle (NT)
Tel: 01929 481294

Corfe Model Village
Tel: 01929 481234; www.
corfecastlemodelvillage.co.uk

Fine Foundation Marine Centre
Purbeck Marine Wildlife
Reserve, Kimmeridge Bay.
Tel: 01929 481044

Kingston Lacy (NT)
Wimborne Minster.
Tel: 01202 883402

Knoll Gardens
Hampreston, near Wimborne.
Tel: 01202 873931;
www.knollgardens.co.uk

Lulworth Castle & Park
East Lulworth, Wareham.
Tel: 0845 450 1054;
www.lulworth.com

Monkey World
Wool, near Wareham.
Tel: 0800 456600;
www.monkeyworld.org

Oceanarium
Pier Approach, West Beach,
Bournemouth.
Tel: 01202 311993;
www.oceanarium.co.uk

Old Poole Lifboat Museum
The Quay, Poole.

Poole Pottery
Sopers Lane, Poole.
Tel: 01202 666200;
www.poolepottery.com

Priest's House Museum & Garden
23–27 High Street,
Wimborne Minster.
Tel: 01202 882533;
www.priest-house.co.uk

Swanage Museum & Heritage Centre
Tel: 01929 421427;
www.swanagemuseum.
org.uk

Swanage Railway
Tel: 01929 425800;
www.swanagerailway.co.uk

Tolpuddle Martyrs' Museum
Tel: 01305 848237

Wareham Town Museum
Town Hall, East Street.
Tel: 01929 533448

Waterfront Museum
Poole.
Tel: 01202 262600

FOR CHILDREN

Adventure Wonderland
Hurn.
Tel: 01202 483444; www.
adventurewonderland.co.uk

Farmer Palmer's
Wareham Road, Organford,
Poole.
Tel: 01202 622022;
www.farmerpalmers.co.uk

Model Town
Wimborne Minster.
Tel: 01202 881924; www.
wimborne-modeltown.com

Splashdown Water Park
Tower Park, northeast of
Poole on A3049.
Tel: 01202 716000;
www.splashdownpoole.com

■ SHOPPING

Poole Markets
Street market, High Street,
and Farmer's Market,
Falkland Square, every Thu.

**Swanage Market & Farmers'
Market**
Main beach car park, Tue,
Easter–Autumn.

Wareham Market
Every Thu.

**Wimborne Market &
Farmers' Market**
Friday; also flea market
Sat–Sun.

■ PERFORMING ARTS

Pavilion Theatre
Westover Road,
Bournemouth.
Tel: 01202 456400

**Bournemouth International
Centre**
Exeter Road.
Tel: 01202 456400

Pier Theatre
Exeter Road, Bournemouth.
Tel: 01202 456 456

■ SPORTS & ACTIVITIES

Adrenalin Days
Tel: 07881 586575.
A variety of powerboat and
charter boat trips that leave
from Poole Harbour.

**Christchurch Ski & Leisure
Centre**
Matchams Lane, Hurn.
Tel: 01202 499155;
www.christchurch-
skicentre.com

Shockwave
Bournemouth Pier.
Tel: 01202 558550;
www.dorsetcruises.co.uk
Speedboat tours of the bay.

CRUISES & FERRIES

Blue Line Cruises
Sailings from Poole Quay.
Tel: 0800 096 0695/
01202 467882;
www.bluelinecruises.co.uk

Brownsea Island Ferries Ltd
Tel: 01929 462383; www.
brownseaislandferries.com

The Dorset Belles
Bournemouth Pier.
Tel: 01202 558550;
www.dorsetcruises.co.uk
Ferry services.

CYCLE HIRE

**First Floor, Dolphin
Shopping Centre, Poole**
Tel: 01202 680123;
www.cycle-paths.co.uk

FISHING

Poole Sea Angling Centre
Rear of 5 High Street, Poole.
Tel: 01202 676597; www.
pooleseaanglingcentre.co.uk

WATERSPORTS

FC Watersports Academy
by Sandbanks Hotel,
Sandbanks, Poole.
Tel: 01202 708283;
www.fcwatersports.co.uk

Rockley Watersports
Rockley Point Sailing Centre,
west of Poole.
Tel: 0870 777 0541;
www.rockleywatersports.com

The Waterboard
14–16 Station Road, Poole.
Tel: 01202 738448;
www.thewaterboard.co.uk

WALKING

**Ghost Walks of Old Poole
Town**
Meet at Scaplen's Court
Museum, Sarum Street.
Tel: 07977 969080

Stour Valley Way
A 64-mile (103km) route
between Christchurch and
Stourhead.

■ ANNUAL EVENTS
& CUSTOMS

Bournemouth
Classic Cars on the Prom.
Sun from 4pm, mid-Apr
to mid-Sep.
Carnival, first week Aug.
Tel: 0771 359 0629; www.
bournemouthcarnival.org.uk

Wimborne
Folk Festival, mid-Jun. www.
wimbornefolkfestival.co.uk

Swanage
Regatta & Carnival Week,
late Jul, early Aug.
www.swanagecarnival.com

Tarrant Hinton
Great Dorset Steam Fair.
Late Aug–early Sep.
Tel: 01258 488928;
www.gdsf.co.uk

Tea Rooms

All Fired Up Café

The Square, 35–37 Bourne Avenue, Bournemouth, BH2 6DT
Tel: 01202 558030;
www.allfiredupceramics.co.uk

This is a café with a huge difference – tuck into herbal, fruit or iced teas, Italian coffee and tasty home-baked cakes, while you decorate your own pottery blank. Your piece will be fully fired and glazed for you to collect a few days later.

Blue Pool and Tea House

Furzebrook, near Wareham, BH20 5AT
Tel: 01929 551408;
www.bluepooluk.com

The Blue Pool is a beauty spot created from an old clay works, surrounded by 25 acres (10ha) of woodland and heath. The genteel Tea House was first opened here in 1935 and boasts its own little museum. Today it serves cream teas and light lunches, and is the perfect stopping place for refreshments as you explore the area.

Worth Café Centre

Worth Matravers, Swanage, BH19 3LQ
Tel: 01929 439360

In the middle of a row of converted stone barns, this cosy café offers a variety of fresh home-made treats such as Dorset apple cake, as well as tempting lunches such as spinach and mushroom bake.

The Courtyard Tea Room

Model Village, The Square, Corfe Castle, BH20 5EZ
Tel: 01929 481234

Home-cooked food is the order of the day at this tea room in the middle of Corfe village. As well as cream teas and cakes, you can tuck into daily lunchtime specials. In fine weather, you can eat out under the shady umbrellas in the 17th-century courtyard.

Pubs

The Bankes Arms Hotel

Watery Lane, Studland, BH19 3AU
Tel: 01929 450225

Once the haunt of smugglers, this creeper-clad old inn is renowned for its large menu of fresh fish and seafood, including fresh mussels, crab gratin and lobster dishes. There are meat options, too, such as lamb noisettes in mint, honey and orange sauce. Each year the pub hosts a beer festival, with around 60 real ales on tap accompanied by music, Morris dancing and stone carving in the garden.

The Castle Inn

Main Road, West Lulworth, BH20 5RN
Tel: 01929 400311

Thatched and beamed, this atmospheric old pub close to Lulworth Cove is perfectly placed for walkers and other visitors. There's an extensive tiered garden, which fills up quickly on summer days, and is especially popular with families. Dogs are permitted too. The menu includes some staples such as chicken, ham and mushroom pie, seafood stew, and fillet steak with oysters. And for something unusual, flambé dishes are cooked at your table. Beers include Ringwood Best.

Langton Arms

Tarrant Monkton, DT11 8RX
Tel: 01258 830225;
www.thelangtonarms.co.uk

This lovely old thatched pub in the centre of the village has a great reputation for its food, and is popular with families year round. The menu changes frequently, but includes tasty treats such as game pie, delicious baked aubergine with ratatouille and mozzarella, and locally made Purbeck ice cream or maybe profiteroles with butterscotch sauce. There's a good-sized beer garden, and a children's play area.

New Forest

ASHURST ■ BEAULIEU ■ BREAMORE ■ BROCKENHURST

BUCKLER'S HARD ■ BURLEY ■ CALSHOT ■ CYCLE RIDE 1

CHRISTCHURCH ■ ELING ■ EXBURY ■ FORDINGBRIDGE ■ FRITHAM

WALK 3 ■ CYCLE RIDE 2 ■ LYMINGTON ■ LYNDHURST

MINSTEAD ■ RINGWOOD ■ ROCKBOURNE ■ WALK 4 ■ WALK 5

FURZEY GARDENS, BEAULIEU

The New Forest, an ancient Royal hunting forest, was created 'new' by William the Conqueror in 1079 as a preserve for hunting deer. The forest is not all dense woodland, as first-time visitors often expect, but consists largely of heathland, with a rich variety of plant life and animals, including the semi-wild ponies, cattle, donkeys and squirrels. Explore beyond the major tourist spots on foot, by bike or on horseback to discover the magic of the place. There are towns, villages and gardens to visit, and attractions include Beaulieu's famous motor museum and the Solent coast.

3 Walk start point

1 Cycle start point

Unmissable attractions

Witness the 'wild' New Forest ponies roaming through woodland and grazing freely on the rough grass with their foals...learn to sail at one of Lymington's busy sailing schools...admire the gardens at Exbury House, famous for its bold rhododendron blooms...power along tracks on a mountain bike or take a leisurely horse-drawn wagon ride at Burley...throw a line in and catch a crab on Mudeford's pretty little quay...stand by the Rufus Stone, the spot where King William II is supposed to have died...bottle-feed a calf or a kid at Longdown Activity Farm...sit quietly in St Nicholas' church at Brockenhurst, the oldest church in the forest...watch fine thoroughbred racehorses galloping across open ground near Roman Rockbourne.

1 Christchurch
The Priory Church has been at the heart of this town for more than 1,200 years, although the present building was begun in the 11th century.

2 Lymington
A leading sailing resort, Lymington has two marinas and is the main port for ferries going to Yarmouth on the Isle of Wight. This lively town with its Georgian and Victorian houses has a great, buzzing atmosphere.

3 Highcliffe Castle
Acquired by the local council in 1977, Highcliffe has undergone much restoration. The first task was to ensure that the structure and roof were secure. Funding from the National Lottery has enabled a massive renovation programme to take place.

4 Cycling in the New Forest
The New Forest Cycle Network links several sites and villages. Most tracks are shared with horse-riders and walkers.

5 Hurst Castle
The castle is one of several defensive southern coast castles erected by Henry VIII. Its low walls were difficult to target from a vessel at sea, and the sturdy structure was able to support heavy artillery.

6 Furzey Gardens
Established in 1922, the lovely gardens incorporate a lake, heathers, and trees and shrubs that give a year-round blaze of colour. The restored Cole Cottage in the grounds dates from the 16th century.

4

5

6

ASHURST MAP REF SU3311

A string of villages lines the A35 between Totton and Lyndhurst. Ashurst, where the housing suddenly stops and the countryside proper begins, was known simply as Lyndhurst Road, like its railway station, until the 1920s, and has developed as prime commuter housing for nearby Southampton. The railway bridge in Ashurst once defined the outer boundary of the New Forest, and this was as close to the hotels and facilities of Lyndhurst that the local landowners would permit the railway to encroach – in fact, the line was forced to take such a circuitous route that it was nicknamed the 'Weymouth Wanderer'. Further on, to the southwest is the popular campsite of Ashurst Woods.

East of Ashurst, Longdown Activity Farm is a hands-on attraction for all ages, including bottle-feeding goat kids, and calves. Close by is the New Forest Otter, Owl and Wildlife Conservation Park – 25 secluded acres (10ha) of ancient woodland where native species are conserved including red squirrels, harvest mice and barn owls.

■ Insight

NEW FOREST PONIES

New Forest ponies may roam freely, but they are not strictly wild – they belong to the commoners. The Victorians 'improved' the hardy ponies that had grazed the forest for centuries, surviving on a diet of gorse, bracken and brambles, by inter-breeding them with Arab stallions – and now they mainly eat grass. Every autumn the ponies are rounded up for branding and marking, and several times a year ponies are sold at Beaulieu Road Station.

BEAULIEU MAP REF SU3802

The pretty little village of Beaulieu has become synonymous with the National Motor Museum, the private passion of the enterprising then Lord Montagu. His forefathers acquired the Beaulieu estate in Tudor times, with its Cistercian abbey founded in 1204.

The abbey was torn down as part of the dissolution of the monasteries countrywide, but the fine cloisters survived and now contain a re-created monastic garden; the refectory became the parish church; and the Domus, the lay brothers' apartments, now houses an exhibition about abbey life. The Tudor house created from the 14th-century gatehouse was reconstructed in the 19th century as the present Palace House, and today shows the domestic workings of a Victorian household. During World War II the estate became the top-secret training school for those involved in the Special Operations Executive (SOE), where agents prepared for operations behind enemy lines in occupied France and Europe, and this story is told in the Secret Army Exhibition.

Lord Montagu first opened this lovely Palace House to the public in 1952, and the brilliant motor museum is dedicated to the memory of his father. It was in fact John Montagu who had successfully petitioned Parliament to abolish the 12mph (19kph) speed limit, among other notable achievements. Today there are more than 250 vintage beauties and stars of the car world to admire in this famous collection, ranging from world record breakers as 'Bluebird' and 'Golden Arrow' to TV favourites including

Mr Bean's green Mini, and James Bond's Lotus submarine car from the movie *The Spy Who Loved Me*. A trip on the 'Wheels' pod ride transports you through a century of motoring history, and you can explore the site on a replica 1912 bus or the high-level monorail. Look out for the special events that take place throughout the year.

BREAMORE MAP REF SU1517

Breamore (pronounced 'Bremmer') is an unspoiled village in the northeast corner of the New Forest, with many attractive redbrick, thatched cottages grouped peacefully around its village green. It's a scene jealously guarded from change, and even the village stocks still stand, opposite the Bat and Ball pub. The little church, which dates from about 1000, is one of the most interesting Saxon survivals in Hampshire. The 12th-century porch contains part of the Saxon rood screen, a fine piece of carving, though the figures have been damaged.

The redbrick Elizabethan manor house of Breamore, built on the hillside in 1583, was purchased by Queen Anne's physician Sir Edward Hulse in the 18th century, and is still a family home with collections of paintings, furniture, needlework and porcelain. The Great Hall contains its original carved stone fireplace, and there is a Victorian kitchen with gleaming copperware. The fascinating Countryside Museum occupies the old farmyard, and has full-size replicas of the village shops that would have made the estate self-sufficient, including a wheelwright's, a blacksmith's and a brewery.

◼ Insight

FLYING BOATS

Before the advent of World War II, the lumbering forms of flying boats were a familiar sight on Southampton Water. They were based at Hythe, a coastal town northeast of Beaulieu, and flew from here to all parts of the British Empire otherwise inaccessible to aircraft. The parent company was Imperial Airways, which was later nationalised as British Overseas Airways Corporation (BOAC).

BROCKENHURST
MAP REF SU3002

Brockenhurst is a big, pleasant village set amid wooded countryside. On the northern outskirts are two of the largest and loveliest of the New Forest 'lawns', Butts Lawn and Balmer Lawn, the latter overlooked by an elegant hotel.

New Forest churches tend to stand aloof from their villages and ancient Brockenhurst's St Nicholas' church, hidden away to the east, is no exception. It is reputedly the oldest in the forest, and it was the only one recorded in the 1086 Domesday survey. The yew tree that almost smothers the building has a girth of more than 20 feet (6m). and is known to be more than 1,000 years old.

To the northwest of Brockenhurst is the Rhinefield Ornamental Drive. It features a variety of coniferous trees, including very large redwoods. Forest walks on either side of the drive include a special 'Tall Trees Walk'. Further on, Bolderwood Drive passes close to the famous ancient Knightwood Oak, and the deer sanctuary where platforms offer a view of deer roaming the forest.

BUCKLER'S HARD

MAP REF SU4000

Two redbrick, terraced rows of Georgian houses face each other across a wide open space that slopes gently down to the Beaulieu River, on the Beaulieu estate. The area is kept free of cars and presents a peaceful rural scene today. Yet Buckler's Hard, originally called Montagu Town, was the shipyard that built many of the men-of-war for Nelson's fleet, including *Agamemnon*, Nelson's favourite ship. The yard was immensely busy, but overreached itself and folded in 1811. During World War II Buckler's Hard revived its shipbuilding tradition, and some parts of a Mulberry Harbour for the D-Day landings were constructed here. The Maritime Museum displays models of many of the ships built here, and reconstructed cottage interiors offer an insight into the life of 18th-century shipyard workers.

Today, pleasure craft ride the tranquil waters of the Beaulieu River and, in summer, cruises set off from the quay. A riverside walk leads to Beaulieu village.

BURLEY MAP REF SU2102

Burley is an excellent centre for walking, horse-riding and mountain biking. It is an attractive village set high above the River Avon amid the bleak and gaunt heathlands of the western New Forest, where ponies and cattle roam freely. Burley Beacon is the high point of the village, reached by the gravel track from Pound Lane, and from its height the view expands westwards over the Avon Valley. Even better is the view from Castle Hill, topped by an Iron Age camp, at nearby Burley Street. Red deer roam in the grounds of grand Burley Manor.

During the 1950s Burley had its own resident witch, called Sybil Leek, who dressed in black robes with a jackdaw perched on her shoulder. Despite her 'white' tendencies, local resentment at her presence caused her to flee to out America. Since then the village has specialised in witchcraft shops as well as the usual range of antiques and other souvenirs. A window in the little church commemorates Constance Applebee, who died in 1981 at the ripe old age of 107. Burley is also home to New Forest Cider, a cider farm with a shop and an exhibition to show how it is made.

CALSHOT MAP REF SU4701

The well-preserved remains of one of Henry VIII's coastal gun-stations, built between 1539 and 1540 against the real threat of a French invasion, stands on a gravel spit jutting out into the Solent. It continued to be of military importance, and today contains a reconstructed barrack room complete with replica 1890s furnishings and a display on the history of the fort. During both world wars it was a Royal Naval Air Station, a base for seaplanes and flying boats, and in the 1920s and 30s the Schneider Trophy seaplane races were held here.

The beach has been designated a country park and adjoins Lepe Country Park to the west, forming a long stretch of shoreline backed by pines and cliff-top walks. The area is known for its habitats – shingle beaches, reed beds, marsh and brackish ponds – which attract extensive marine and bird life.

A New Forest loop from Burley

This route takes you through the heart of the bustling New Forest village of Burley, with its antiques shops, tea rooms and horse-drawn wagon rides then joins the Castleman cycle trail where you can experience the surrounding heathland from a level stretch of old railway line. There are good opportunities for birdwatching, and you can visit the Old Station tea rooms at Holmsley.

Route Directions

1 Turn right out of the car park, stop at the next road junction, and then continue straight ahead. Fork left at the war memorial into Pound Lane, which is signed to Bransgore. Cycle past the Forest Teahouse and cider shop, then follow the lane out over the heath until you get to Burbush Hill.

2 Fork left just before the old railway bridge, following the waymarked off-road cycle track through the Forestry Commission's car park and down on to the old railway line. The Castleman Trail sets out from a lovely sandy cutting, which is smothered with brilliant purple heather in late summer. Soon the old line emerges from the cutting onto a low embankment, with good views out over the boggy heath. You'll often see horse riders in the area and birdwatchers should look out for green woodpeckers, as well as for lapwings, curlews and redshanks, which nest on the heath in early summer. The trail rises briefly to the broken brickwork of Greenberry Bridge, which survived the closure of the railway, only to be demolished in 1995 when it became unsafe. Continue to the low wooden barriers that guard the minor road crossing at Holmsley Passage, where you can still see short sections of the original railway lines that are embedded in the road.

3 If you wish, you can shorten the ride by turning left here. To complete the full route, cross the road and continue along the old railway line. The trail becomes more shaded as it runs perfectly straight through an avenue of young oak trees. The track crosses two small bridges that herald the approach to Holmsley Station. Look out for the old brick platform on your right before dismounting at the wooden gate that marks the end of the cycle track.

4 Beyond the gate and across the road, the Old Station Tea Rooms are well worth a visit for morning coffee, tasty home-cooked lunches and delicious cream teas. There's a pleasant garden, as well as a gift shop where you can buy a souvenir of your visit to this unusual refreshment stop. Turn here and retrace your outward route to Holmsley Passage (Point 3). Turn right on to the quiet lane. Follow the lane up the hill and then stop at the 5-way junction.

5 Cross straight over towards Burley Lawn and zig-zag left, then right, past The White Buck Inn into Bennetts Lane.

6 Bear left when you reach the next junction leading into Beechwood Lane and keep straight on through Lester Square until you reach a T-junction. Turn left here towards Burley, and continue past the little brick-built church of St John the Baptist for the final 400yds (366m) back to the car park.

Route facts

DISTANCE/TIME 6 miles (9.7km) 1h

MAP OS OS Explorer OL22 New Forest

START Public car park, (fee) Burley, grid ref: SU 211030

TRACKS Busy village centre, quiet lanes and an old railway route

GETTING TO THE START
Burley village is on a minor road southeast of Ringwood, between the A31 and the A35. Leave the A31 at Picket Post, 1 mile (1.6km) east of Ringwood, and follow the signposted route through Burley Street to Burley. Keep left at the war memorial in the centre of the village, and you'll find The Queens Head immediately on your left, with the public car park entrance just beyond the pub's own car park.

THE PUB The Queens Head, The Cross, Burley, Ringwood. Tel: 01425 403423

❶ Burley's streets get busy at weekends and during holiday periods. Good traffic sense required.

CHRISTCHURCH MAP REF SZ1892

This ancient town lies on the south coast where the rivers Stour and Avon pour their waters into the bay. At the time of the Domesday survey there were a mere 21 houses here, and it was then named Twynham. The church was started later in the 11th century, and became an Agustinian priory around 1150. Today all that remains is the Priory Church, which looms gold above the town, and is well worth exploring inside for its carvings in both stone and wood. Look out for the Norman turret in the north transept, and the superb carving of the Salisbury Chantry. Nearby Place Mill, mentioned in the Domesday Book, was used for fulling (cleaning and thickening cloth) and corn grinding until 1808, and now has displays of old milling items, with an art and crafts gallery upstairs.

One of Christchurch town's most unusual sights is its surviving ducking stool, reached via a flagged alleyway beside the Olde George Inn – a wooden stool on the end of a pole which can be swung out into the chilly millstream, in a scolds' punishment revived with good humour in 1986. The town's Red House Museum is a collection of local and natural history, housed in an appealing old Georgian house with a lovely garden.

Across the wide estuary, the pastel coloured nostalgic beach huts in rows on Mudeford's sandy peninsula are a cheerful throwback to childhood bucket-and-spade holidays of the early 20th century. This windswept peninsula has an archaeological record dating back 12,500 years, when Stone Age hunter-gatherers left the remains of a campsite on its outer, seaward edge. Some 10,500 years later, Iron Age folk had settled here and built up a good trading port on the inner shore, where Barn Field stands today. The great Double Dikes date from this period, built to shelter a village of timber-framed dwellings.

Barn Field itself has remained untouched by farming improvements since the Romans left in around AD 410 – a rare status jealously protected by conservationists. It's an area of low, acid grassland gripping onto thin soil over gravel and sand, maintained down the centuries by the salt-laden winds and the sharp teeth of the rabbit population. Decimation of the rabbits in the 1950s by myxomatosis allowed gorse and bramble to gain a hold, but a recent programme of scrub clearance and controlled grazing by cattle, managed by English Nature, has done much to restore the original balance. Today it is an important site for ground-nesting birds such as the skylark and meadow pipit, and adorned with heath bedstraw, autumn hawkbit and harebell.

ELING MAP REF SU3612

The Saxon village of Eling, on a little tidal creek off Southampton Water, was a shipbuilding village until the end of the 19th century. Before that it was a small port from where Henry I is said to have sailed to Normandy in 1130.

The creek, a sheltered little harbour for sailing craft, is crossed by a fast causeway with sluice gates to hold back the high tides and, in the little building on the northern shore, the power of Southampton Water's famous double

tides is harnessed and used to produce wholemeal flour. Eling Tide Mill is the only surviving tide mill regularly milling pure stoneground flour. The Domesday Book of 1086 records a mill here, but the present building dates from the 18th century. It was restored in 1980 and milling demonstrations are given, depending on the tides. You can learn more about Eling and neighbouring Totton in the heritage centre by the mill.

The causeway across the creek at Eling carries the only remaining toll road in Hampshire, which has been in operation since at least 1418.

EXBURY MAP REF SU4300

This pleasant estate village nestling on the Beaulieu River is famed for the fine magnificent rhododendron gardens at Exbury House. They were the creation of banker Lionel de Rothschild, whose passion was gardening – and he gardened on a magnificent scale. Rothschild started here in the 1920s, with 600 acres (243ha) of wooded slopes overlooking the peaceful river, which he split into 250 acres (101ha) of gardens and 350 acres (142ha) of arboretum. He imported more than 1,000 varieties of rhododendron, then created 452 more by careful crossing. Today the gardens are run by his son, Edmund. The mild climate of the Beaulieu River valley ensures a long flowering season, with breathtaking displays between April and June. Camellias, azaleas and magnolias contribute a great deal to the glory of an Exbury spring. Other 'gardens' on the site include a daffodil meadow, rock garden, rose garden and water garden. A miniature steam railway offers a 20-minute tour of the Summer Lane Garden, leading to the American Garden. Dogs on a short lead are welcome.

FORDINGBRIDGE
MAP REF SU1514

Fordingbride stands at a shallow point on the River Avon, and is known as the northern gateway of the New Forest. It grew up around the light industries of pottery, brick-making and canvas sailcloth weaving, and has roots that date back to the Domesday survey and beyond. Branksome China, located on Shaftesbury Street, continues the old tradition of porcelain manufacture and hand painting, offering tours and a shop.

The town's elegant 14th-century bridge has seven arches, so solid in their stonework that they were drilled only with great difficulty during World War II by Royal Engineers, who were inserting explosives ready to blow the bridge up in the event of enemy invasion.

■ Visit

SOLDIER BROTHERS' MEMORIAL

In Exbury's Church of St Catherine is a fine bronze memorial by Cecil Thomas to John and Alfred Forster, brothers who were killed in World War I. It shows a soldier's effigy lying on a tomb, and is impressively lifelike, down to the folds in the greatcoat and the lacing-up of the boots. The young sculptor was wounded in the war, and while in hospital met and befriended Lt Alfred Forster of the Royal Scots Greys, who later died of his wounds. After the war, Lord and Lady Forster commissioned Thomas to design a memorial to Alfred and his brother.

Despite the destruction of much of the old town by fire in 1702, there are around 70 listed buildings scattered through Fordingbridge, and a town walk takes you past many of the best. St Mary's Church is notable for the fine 15th-century carved roof in the north chancel chapel, and for its Miracle Stone on the outer wall of the north chapel. The Fordingbridge Museum includes an exhibition about the artist Augustus John, as well as artefacts to illustrate tales of smuggling in the town and many other curiosities.

South of the town off the A338, at South Gorley, Hockey's Farm is an open-air farming museum, with interesting fossil displays, a deer park, and a farm shop well stocked with home-produced beef and lamb, sausages, cakes and home-cured bacon.

FRITHAM MAP REF SU2314

The isolated rural hamlet of Fritham lies to the north of the A31. The plains to the south were used as an airfield during World War II, and to the north you'll find the lonely settlement, perhaps founded by squatters, known as Nomansland. The village inn, the Royal Oak, is a small traditional country pub, with few frills. Snug under its thatched roof, it is a reminder of a simple age when pigs snuffled in the woods, each home had a cow or two and some hens, services in the tiny tin chapel were held twice on Sundays attended by all, and the main road out was a grassy track.

Between 1863 and 1921, Fritham's fortunes changed and the village thrived as the base for an extensive gunpowder

■ Insight

ROYAL HUNTING GROUND

William the Conqueror created the New Forest as a preserve for deer, regarded from early times as the true sporting beasts of kings. Forest Law was severe and enforced to maintain the best possible environment for the 'beasts of the chase'. Today there are five species of deer in the forest, of which the most numerous are fallow deer. They are managed by the New Forest keepers, employed by the Forestry Commission. Of all the deer in the forest, the white buck, a rare albino form, was the most favoured. Legend has it that Henry VIII and his courtiers once chased a white buck quite a way through the forest towards Ringwood, and that he spared its life at the request of the ladies. Today the 'White Hart' appears on many an inn sign.

factory. The factory made use of locally produced charcoal and water from a chalybeate spring, still known as Irons Well. After the factory closed down, Fritham returned to a quieter existence.

At Canterton Glen, to the southeast of Fritham, lies the Rufus Stone, a small memorial marking the place where King William II (known as William Rufus), met his untimely death in 1100. King William loved hunting, and was killed by an arrow supposedly intended for a deer. The Rufus Stone is said to mark the spot, but some say it was much nearer Bolderwood, or Stoney Cross, or Fritham itself. Some question whether the King's death was an accident. Whatever the truth, his brother Henry rode straight to Winchester to be proclaimed king, while William's body was carried there on the cart of a charcoal burner.

A Forest Walk from Fritham

A walk from a hidden hamlet and the site of a former gunpowder factory, through woodland and open heathland. As you make your way through the peaceful mixed woodlands, look out for nests of wood ants beside the tracks, the mounds will be feverish with activity on dry warm days, and listen for the distinctive 'yaffle' of the green woodpecker, a common forest bird that feeds on the wood ants.

Route Directions

1 Turn left out of the car park and head downhill along the road. The road eventually becomes gravelled and then passes Eyeworth Pond to the right. Continue past Eyeworth Cottage and Eyeworth Lodge, then take the footpath on the right beyond Oak Tree Cottage at the end of the track.

2 Bear off to the left and then, at a fork, keep left through the trees close to the field boundary. As the boundary swings further left, bear right along a track between tall coniferous and deciduous woods. At a T-junction by a large single fir, turn left along a grassy track. Cross a ford and walk up to a junction.

3 Turn right on to a gravel track and then, where it bears sharply to the right, keep ahead with the grassy track. Ascend into more open countryside and continue to climb along the meandering path, ignoring paths left and right, across the edge of Fritham Plain. The path bears right towards the trees to a track. Turn left, then right and enter Sloden Inclosure.

4 Walk through the Inclosure, then descend across open heathland towards a cottage. Cross a bridge and bear right and then, just before Holly Hatch Cottage, turn left through a gate. At a fork, bear right along a grassy track and gently climb through Holly Hatch Inclosure to reach a gravel track.

5 Turn left, then in about 400yds (366m), turn right at a major junction and shortly reach a gate on the woodland edge. Turn left here, on to a wide track beside the wood, then keep left at a fork. The track soon becomes concrete and then passes to the right of Cadmans Pool. Cross over a metalled road and take a left turn along a grassy track to enter more woodland.

6 In 50yds (46m), turn right, with the trees giving way to gorse bushes and grassland. As the footpath becomes indistinct, maintain direction and soon bear left on to the gravel track. Continue to a gate and walk across an area of concrete, taking the path in the bottom right-hand corner that leads down into South Bentley Inclosure.

7 Walk downhill to a gate (numbered 75) and turn right. Cross a stream (there is a ford) and keep ahead along an indistinct path, soon to bear half-left through a copse to reach a larger stream. Walk along the right-hand bank and cross the wooden bridge.

8 Continue ahead, the path passing a house and gate to become a gravelled drive. Keep to the drive until you reach the junction by The Royal Oak pub and turn left back to the car park.

Route facts

DISTANCE/TIME
6 miles (9.6km) 3h

MAP OS Outdoor Leisure 22 New Forest

START Forestry Commission car park beyond Royal Oak pub, grid ref: SU 230141

TRACKS Gravel forest tracks, heathland and woodland paths

GETTING TO THE START
Fritham lies just off the A31 between Ringwood and Southampton, with easy access from the M27. At Stoney Cross turn off the A31 towards Fritham. After 2km take the second left, entering the village, then turn left again, following through the village until you reach the car park on your left.

THE PUB The Royal Oak, Fritham. Tel: 02380 812606

❶ Getting lost in the New Forest is deceptively easy so make sure you carry the necessary maps and guide information with you.

A circuit around Linwood

This relatively remote ride offers a good chance of some peace and quiet, and the opportunity to see the New Forest at its best. You'll follow the waymarked Forestry Commission off-road cycle tracks deep into the heart of the Forest for the majority of the ride, with two short sections on tarred roads where you will need to watch out for the occasional car. There are opportunities for birdwatching or, alternatively, for studying other local wildlife as you go through a variety of terrain. You are highly likely to see deer along this trail, especially if you come here early in the morning or at around dusk – go quietly for the best chance of seeing these timid woodland residents in their natural habitat.

Route Directions

1 Turn right out of the car park and continue straight on, passing the end of the gravel track that leads up to The High Corner Inn.

2 At Woodford Bottom bear left at the wooden barrier on your right and pass the ford across the Dockens Water stream, also on your right.

Keep to the waymarked cycle route as it closely follows the gravelled track that winds across the open heath, past a few scattered houses and the tree-capped mound of Black Barrow. A few smaller tracks lead off to left and right, but the main gravelled trail is easy enough to follow. Keep straight on as a similar track leads in from your left near the thatched Bogmyrtle Cottage, until you join a tarred lane. Almost at once the lane turns sharp left through a tiny ford and climbs gently up to the road junction at The Red Shoot Inn.

3 Turn left opposite the post-box, still following the waymarked cycle route, and continue to climb until the road levels off and swings to the left at Amie's Corner. Fork right here, sticking with the waymarked cycle route as it joins a gravelled forest track. The trail dives into Milkham Inclosure through wooden gates beside an attractive whitewashed cottage, then drops to a bridge over the Linford Brook.

4 A few yards further on turn left at the numbered waymark post 5, then follow the track as it winds through open mixed woodland and then re-crosses the Linford Brook. Continue as the track bears right at the next waymark post, then right again in front of a pair of wooden gates where you enter an area of

mainly coniferous woodland. Another pair of wooden gates punctuates your progress to the top of the hill, where further gates lead you out into the Forestry Commission's Milkham car park. Go through here, cross the car park, and stop at the road junction.

5 Turn left towards Linwood and follow the narrow tarred lane for 500yds (457m) until it bears away to the left. Fork right here on to the waymarked cycle trail that follows the gravel track towards Broomy Lodge and Holly Hatch. Here your route crosses the high heathland plateau of Broomy Plain. This is a good spot to see Dartford warblers, meadow pipits and stonechats, and you'll also enjoy good long views towards Cranborne Chase and the Wiltshire Downs. Bear right at the next fork and then follow the trail down into Holly Hatch Inclosure.

6 At the foot of the hill, numbered waymark post 3 stands at the forest cross-roads. Turn left here, on to a lovely tree-shaded track with soft green verges that leads you through the oak woods. Two pairs of wooden gates mark your progress through the inclosure, and at length the oaks give way to conifers.

Route facts

DISTANCE/TIME 7 miles (11.3km) 1h45

MAP OS OS Explorer OL22 New Forest

START Spring Bushes car park, Linwood, grid ref: SU 196107

CYCLE HIRE Country Lanes, 9 Shaftesbury Street, Fordingbridge. Tel: 01425 655022

TRACKS Gravelled forest tracks, two short sections on rural lanes

GETTING TO THE START Linwood is a village on a minor road northeast of Ringwood. Spring Bushes car park is on the road that runs west from Emery Down, near Lyndhurst, to Rockford, just north of Ringwood.

THE PUB The High Corner Inn, Linwood. Tel: 01425 473973

❶ Moderate hills, some uneven and stony tracks. Suitable for older children, some off-road riding experience useful.

Follow the waymarked trail until you rejoin your outward route at a low wooden barrier. Turn left here, and climb the short hill back to The High Corner Inn.

NO MOORING LANDING ONLY

LYMINGTON MAP REF SZ3295

Lymington is a busy sailing town at the mouth of the Lymington River. It received its charter in 1200 and became a free port, flourishing as the closest mainland harbour to the Isle of Wight, to which ferries still run. In the Middle Ages Lymington rivalled Southampton as a major port – and the numerous creeks around here were much frequented by smugglers well into the 18th century. Today the tidal salt marshes stretch for 10 miles (16km), and are protected as a national nature reserve.

For many years the town's prosperity depended on the production of salt, but sadly this trade eventually died out and Lymington briefly became a fashionable bathing place. By the end of the 19th century it had really developed as a sailing centre, and today the town has an excellent yacht basin and is the headquarters of two sailing clubs. There is boat building too and, as with many ports, it is famed for its inns – reputedly there were once 45.

The wide Georgian and Victorian High Street, which climbs the hill from the quay to the church, bursts into life on Saturdays when there is a vibrant 700-year-old market, with a great variety of stalls laid out along both sides of the street. Enjoy the view from the hilltop back down across the river, then take a look at the Church of St Thomas, which looks 18th century, with its jaunty white cupola and galleried interior, but is actually medieval. The town's St Barbe Museum is dedicated to the history of the New Forest coast, including hands-on displays for children, while its art gallery offers an ever changing range of exhibitions of world-class artworks.

To the north of Lymington is lovely Spinners, a beautiful woodland garden showing rhododendrons, magnolias, Japanese maples and much more. To the south, on Hurst Spit, stands Hurst Castle, one of Henry VIII's defences and part of the modern coastal artillery defences until 1956.

LYNDHURST MAP REF SU3008

The 'Capital of the New Forest' is quite a sizeable town, and is the only one located within the historical confines of the forest. It was formerly designated the New Forest's administrative centre in 1079 by William I, and it continues to be the official seat of the ancient Court of Verderers whose aim is to protect the rights of the commoners. The Court Room and the Forestry Commission offices are both housed in the beautiful 17th-century Queen's House, and the Verderers meet here every two months. All New Forest animals are under their jurisdiction, while the patrolling of the forest is in the hands of four 'Agisters' – a medieval word meaning 'collector'. The Forestry Commission manages the woodland of the New Forest.

Lyndhurst is a town of narrow streets leading off the main High Street, which snarls up with traffic during peak holiday times. It is full of tourist shops and eating places, with Victorian and Edwardian architecture to admire. The church, on the site of two earlier ones, dominates the High Street with its 160-foot (49m) spire and dates from 1860. It contains windows by Burne-Jones and a

■ Activity

THE HAMPSHIRE AVON

The River Avon rises to the east of Devizes and flows southwards for 48 miles (77km) to the English Channel at Christchurch. In its upper chalky reaches it is a noted trout stream, but where it flows into Hampshire past Breamore and Fordingbridge the acid soils of the New Forest change its nature and it becomes a river for coarse fishing. Below Ringwood it is renowned for salmon. The waymarked Avon Valley Path follows the river for 34 miles (54.5km) from Salisbury to Christchurch.

fresco, *The Parable of the Virgins*, by Lord Leighton. In the village churchyard lies Mrs Hargreaves, who died in 1934. As the little Alice Liddell, she was the real inspiration for Lewis Caroll's *Alice in Wonderland*. The town is the home of the New Forest Visitor Centre and Museum.

Lyndhurst's central position makes it an ideal base for exploring the forest which still presses up close to the town's boundaries,. To the west of Lyndhurst is the picturesque thatched hamlet of Swan Green, formerly the site of an important pony fair, and Emery Down, famed for its Portuguese fireplace, which stands alone in the open air. It was constructed of cobble stones on the site of a building that was occupied by Portuguese troops during World War I, and serves as a memorial to them. The New Forest Reptile Centre, a conservation and education centre dedicated to rare native species, is near by. To the east is Bolton's Bench, an excellent starting point for walks over White Moor Heath.

In summer an open-topped City Sightseeing bus, with space for bicycles, runs every hour from Lyndhurst, and makes 13 stops at key points which include Lymington and Beaulieu.

MINSTEAD MAP REF SU2811

Minstead consists of clusters of cottages amidst trees and pastures, centred on the inn and the church. The latter is of curious construction, having the outward appearance of an old house, all gables and dormers. This is the result of successive 'updates' by local builders who had little idea of ecclesiastical construction, reflecting the unhurried days when the forest turned in on itself and knew little of the world beyond. The interior has rows of box pews and a plethora of galleries. Sir Arthur Conan Doyle (1867–1930), whose most famous literary creation was the detective Sherlock Holmes, lies buried here.

To the northwest of the village lies Furzey Gardens, renowned among many botanists and horticulturists, comprising 8 acres (3ha) of informal planting, which includes azaleas, rhododendrons, ferns, heathers and Chilean fire trees. Within the garden are a thatched Tudor cottage, a crafts gallery and an art gallery.

RINGWOOD MAP REF SU1505

Ringwood is a venerable town on the River Avon, and anglers come from miles around for the coarse and salmon fishing of this reach. This busy centre has always been the New Forest's market town, with its modern buildings blending well with the Georgian houses and older cottages.

There is a good modern shopping centre, and the attractive High Street has traditional shops including fishing tackle suppliers and a gunsmith. The Ringwood Brewery has an outlet on Christchurch Road. In West Street stands Monmouth House, where the Duke of Monmouth was held after his defeat at Sedgemoor in 1685, before being sent to London for execution.

Learn more about the history of the area at the Ringwood Town & Country Experience, a heritage centre to the north of the A31, with reconstructed Victorian shop interiors, a fabulous carousel, and one of the bouncing bombs, developed nearby for the RAF 'Dambusters' in World War II. The Moors Valley Country Park at Ashley Heath offers walks and cycle trails, and other attractions, including a narrow-guage steam railway near to the visitor centre.

To the south of Ringwood, at Crow, is Liberty's Raptor and Reptile Centre, named after a star attraction – an American bald eagle. There are lots of birds of prey, including eagles, hawks, owls and vultures, which take part in regular flying displays, and reptiles such as giant tortoises, snakes and lizards.

ROCKBOURNE MAP REF SU1118

The village of Rockbourne, on the high chalklands northwest of Fordingbridge, is one of Hampshire's prettiest villages, with thatched cottages dating back to Tudor and Georgian times nestling beside a stream in a valley bottom. On the downs above the village are the remains of three barrows: Grans, Knapp and Duck's Nest Long Barrow.

Rockbourne's real fame, however, rests on the Roman villa discovered to the south of the village by a farmer in 1942, when he was digging out a ferret. The villa was a large courtyard type of mansion, possibly part of an imperial estate, with more than 70 rooms, several bath suites, farm houses and work-shops. It was occupied from the mid-2nd century AD until the collapse of Roman rule in the early 5th century. Although much of it has been excavated it has to some extent been backfilled for its own protection, since the site is not under cover, but several mosaics may be seen as you walk around.

As well as the villa, there was a small settlement and a probable cattle enclosure on Rockbourne Down, while nearby Bokerley Dyke, a late Roman earthwork, acts as a local boundary. The museum attached to the villa has pottery, jewellery and elaborate iron work, a large coin hoard and two Roman milestones. Found in the fabric of the villa, where they had been re-used as building material, the milestones date from the reigns of Trajan Decius (AD 249–51) and Tetricus II (AD 272).

Insight

HORSE FLESH

To the northeast of Rockbourne lies the peaceful village of Whitsbury. It is home to the Whitsbury Manor Stud, one of the most successful horse breeding, training and racing stables in Britain. The open downland surrounding the village provides an ideal training ground for potential winners. Racehorses Desert Orchid and Rhyme and Reason were both bred here.

New Forest trails around Bank

Ancient oaks, towering conifers and historic inclosures (different areas of managed woodlands where young trees are protected from deer and ponies) are on the route. Soon after beginning the longer walk you'll pass the most famous and probably the oldest tree in the forest, the Knightwood Oak. It is thought to be at least 350 years old and owes its age to pollarding its limbs to encourage new branches for fuel.

Route Directions

1 Take the gravel path at the top end of the car park (to the right of 'The Tall Trees Trail' sign), parallel with the road.

In 100yds (91m) turn right and descend to a gravel track. Cross straight over then, where it curves left, keep

ahead to a gate and the A35. Cross over, go through a gate and keep to the track, heading uphill to a junction. Turn right and then follow the path to a road. Cross into Knightwood Oak car park and follow the signs leading to the Knightwood Oak itself.

2 From the oak bear right down a wide ride. Go through a gate and keep to the path through more open woodland and bear right towards the A35. Just before a gate and the A35 take the narrow path on the left. Cross a footbridge and turn left and continue along the line of a drainage ditch. Maintain this direction to a cottage. After this, turn left to reach the New Forest Reptile Centre.

3 Walk back along the access drive, passing Holiday Hills Cottage. After 300yds (274m), at a barrier on your left, drop down on to a path and follow it across a bridge.

4 Keep to the main path across several clearings, and at the top of a rise fork right. In 25yds (23m) turn to the right, ultimately descending to and skirting left around cottages and Allum Green. Gently climb through trees to a defined crossing of paths and turn right. Shortly, bear half-right across a clearing and concrete footbridge, then continue forwards through the woodland edge to get to a

telegraph pole. Bear right for 50yds (46m), then left through a gate to the A35.

5 Turn left, then almost immediately right across the road to a gate. Walk straight ahead to a garden boundary and then turn right – the narrow path leads onto a lane in Bank. Turn right, pass The Oak Inn and walk through and up out of the hamlet. Just before you reach a sharp left-hand bend (by a cattle-grid), bear off right beside a barrier and walk straight ahead on a wide path.

6 Go through the patch of trees and scrub to a fork on the edge of a clearing. Keep right to follow the path between an oak and a holly tree. Follow the path until you go past a pretty cottage and along the drive to a metalled lane at Gritnam.

7 Turn left, and after 100yds (91m), before a bridge, turn right to a telegraph pole. Follow the path and turn left along the gravel track to the water treatment works. Keep to its left and continue on into a patch of thicker woodland (mainly birch). The woods soon become more open. Cross a footbridge and then immediately turn left. After about 25yds (23m) fork right.

Route facts

DISTANCE/TIME
5 miles (8km) 3h00

MAP OS Outdoor Leisure 22 New Forest

START Brock Hill Forestry Commission car park, grid ref: SU 266057

TRACK Grass and gravel forest tracks, heathland paths, some roads

GETTING TO THE START Look for signs to the Rhinefield Ornamental Drive, just off the A35 Lyndhurst-to-Christchurch road, some 3 miles (4.8km) southwest of Lyndhurst. Parking is signposted on the right, a short distance off the A35.

THE PUB The Oak Inn, Pinkney Lane, Bank. Tel: 023 8028 2350

❶ Extreme caution needed when crossing the busy A35 (twice). Blind bends on the lane through Bank. Follow directions carefully – unsigned paths, tracks and forest rides.

8 Walk through Brinken Wood and across a clearing to a bridge over Warwickslade Cutting. Bear right, go through a gate and turn sharp right at the gravel track. Swing left back to get to Brock Hill car park.

Around Roman Rockbourne

Through rolling fields and areas of dense woodland, this walk discovers Rockbourne, a gem of a place that has one of the prettiest village high streets in Hampshire and is also home to one of the most interesting Roman villa complexes in the country. You can stop here to see the remains of the villa, its heating system and beautiful mosaics. The walk route continues to the neighbouring village of Whitsbury, where foundations of another Roman building, containing a hypocaust and New Forest pottery dating back to the 2nd and 3rd century AD, were found overlaying earlier, Iron Age settlements on a hill-fort.

Route Directions

1 Turn left out of the car park and take the lane on your right towards Manor Farm. Turn right, signed to the church, and cross the gravel drive to a stepped path to St Andrew's Church. Continue along the right-hand edge of the churchyard to a junction of paths. Keep straight on behind houses, ignoring two paths right, then cross a stile and turn immediately right through a gate.

2 Follow the field edge down to a junction of paths. Keep on the left to a gate and maintain direction across two stiles and along the field edge to a stile in the corner. Climb the stile immediately right and bear left along the edge of a meadow to a stile. Pass in front of a thatched cottage to a stile and track, opposite Marsh Farm.

3 Bear left, then right through a gate and keep to the left through pasture to another gate. Bear half-right to a gate in the corner and proceed along the field edge, eventually reaching a stile and lane. To visit the Roman Villa, turn right to get to a T-junction, and turn right, then left into the entrance. Retrace your steps.

4 Once you are back at the lane, cross over onto a track and then, further along in a copse, at a junction of several tracks, take the arrowed path left up a steep bank into a field. Keep to the left-hand edge and head across a field to a track. Turn right, then left downhill and through the edge of some woodland. Pass a house to enter a lane.

5 Turn right, then left along a bridleway, and gently climb through Radnall Wood. At a fork of paths, bear left (follow the blue arrow) and pass behind Whitsbury House to a lane. Turn left, then right along a track between a few properties to a lane. Turn right, then bear off right along the bridleway taking you through Whitsbury Wood.

6 At a junction with a track, bear left and walk beside paddocks to a bungalow. Turn left along a track between paddocks towards Whitsbury church. Now turn left at the T-junction and shortly enter the churchyard. Go through the gate opposite the church door and descend to the lane.

7 Turn left for The Cartwheel Inn, otherwise turn right, then turn left along a farm drive and keep ahead, bearing left, then right between paddocks, uphill to a gate. Turn turn left along the field edge and then head across the field where you will come to a track.

8 Turn right and follow the track left to a junction of a few tracks. Step over the stile opposite and walk back to Rockbourne church. Retrace steps back to the village hall.

Route facts

DISTANCE/TIME
4.5 miles (7.2km) 1h45

MAP OS Outdoor Leisure 22 New Forest or OS Explorer 130 Salisbury & Stonehenge

START Rockbourne village hall car park, grid ref: SU 113184

TRACKS Field paths, woodland bridleways and tracks, 9 stiles

GETTING TO THE START Take the A338 south from Salisbury. At Fordingbridge take the B3078 west through Sandleheath and follow the signs to Rockbourne village.

THE PUB The Rose & Thistle, Rockbourne. Tel: 01725 518236

■ TOURIST INFORMATION CENTRES

Fordingbridge
Kings Yard, Salisbury Street.
Tel: 01425 654560;
www.visitfordingbridge.com

Christchurch
49 High Street.
Tel: 01202 471780;
www.christchurchtourism.info

Lyndhurst
New Forest Visitor
Information Centre,
Main Car Park.
Tel: 023 8028 2269;
www.thenewforest.co.uk

■ PLACES OF INTEREST

Apple Court Garden & Nursery
Hordle Lane, Hordle,
Lymington.
Tel: 01590 642130;
www.applecourt.com

Beaulieu: National Motor Museum, Palace House, Beaulieu Abbey
Tel: 01590 612123;
www.beaulieu.co.uk

Bolderwood Deer Platform
Signed from Bolderwood car
park. Fallow deer fed here.
www.forestry.gov.uk/newforest

Branksome China
Fordingbridge.
Tel: 01425 652010;
www.branksomechina.co.uk

Breamore Manor House & Countryside Museum
Tel: 01725 512468;
www.breamorehouse.com

Buckler's Hard
Tel: 01590 616203;
www.bucklershard.co.uk

Calshot Fort (EH)
Tel: 02380 892023

Christchurch Priory Church
Quay Road, Christchurch.
Tel: 01202 485804;
www.christchrchpriory.org

Eling Tide Mill
The Toll Bridge, Eling, Totton.
Tel: 023 8086 9575;
www.elingtidemill.org.uk

Exbury Gardens & Steam Railway
Near Beaulieu.
Tel: 023 8089 1203;
www.exbury.co.uk

Fordingbridge Museum
King's Yard, Fordingbridge.
Tel: 01425 655222; www.
fordingbridgemuseum.co.uk

Furzey Gardens
Minstead.
Tel: 023 8081 2464;
www.furzey-gardens.org

Hockey's Farm
South Gorley.
Tel: 01425 652542. Free.

Hurst Castle
Hurst Point, by Keyhaven.
Tel: 01590 642344;
www.hurst-castle.co.uk
Accessible on foot, or
by boat from Keyhaven
(Tel: 01590 642500).

Moors Valley Country Park
Ashley Heath, Ringwood.
Tel: 01425 470721

New Forest Cider
Littlemead, Pound Lane,

Burley.
Tel: 01425 403589;
www.newforestcider.co.uk

New Forest Museum
Main car park, High street,
Lyndhurst.
Tel: 023 8028 3444;
www.newforestmuseum.org.uk

New Forest Reptile Centre
Emery Down.
Tel: 023 8028 3141;
www.forestry.gov.uk/newforest

Place Mill
Quay Road, Christchurch.
Tel: 01202 487626;
www.visitchristchurch.info

Red House Museum
Quay Road, Christchurch.
Tel: 01202 482860

Ringwood Brewery Store
138 Christchurch Road,
Ringwood.
Tel: 01425 471177;
www.ringwoodbrewery.co.uk

Rockbourne Roman Villa
Tel: 01725 518541;
www.hants.gov.uk/museum
/rockbourne

St Barbe Museum and Art Gallery
New Street, Lymington.
Tel: 01590 676969;
www.stbarbe-museum.org.uk

Sammy Miller Motorcycle Museum & Farm Trust
New Milton.
Tel: 01425 620777;
www.sammymiller.co.uk

Spinners Garden & Nursery
Boldre, by Lymington.
Tel: 01590 673347

FOR CHILDREN

Burley Park Deer Safari
Burley Park, Burley.
Tel: 07801 345264;
www.newforestsafari.co.uk

Liberty's Raptor and Reptile Centre
Crow Lane, Crow.
Tel: 01425 476487;
www.libertyscentre.co.uk

Longdown Activity Farm
South of A35, near Ashurst.
Tel: 023 8029 3326;
www.longdownfarm.co.uk

New Forest Otter, Owl and Wildlife Conservation Park
Longdown, near Ashurst.
Tel: 023 8029 2408;
www.ottersandowls.co.uk

Paultons Park
Ower, near Romsey.
Tel: 023 8081 4455;
www.paultonspark.co.uk

SHOPPING

Farmers' Markets
Held in towns throughout the New Forest. Markets take place on alternate Sundays in Beaulieu, Lymington, Lyndhurst and Fordingbridge. Tel: 023 8028 5185; www. forestfriendlyfarming.org.uk.

Christchurch Market
High Street, every Mon.

Lyburn Farmhouse Cheesemakers
Lyburn Farm, Landford, Wiltshire.
Tel: 01794 390451;
www.lyburncheese.co.uk

SPORTS & ACTIVITIES

Go Ape!
Moors Valley Country Park, Horton Road, Ashley Heath.
Tel: 0870 458 9063;
www.goape.co.uk
High-wire forest adventure.

BOATING

Beaulieu River cruises
From Buckler's Hard, 3 miles (4.5km) south of Beaulieu.

Liquid Logistics
Tel: 01590 624730;
www.liquidlogistics.co.uk
Canoeing and kayaking.

Mudeford Ferry Adventure Voyages
Mudeford Quay.
Tel: 01202 488662;
www.adventurevoyages.co.uk

CYCLE HIRE

AA Bike Hire
Fernglen, Gosport Lane, Lyndhurst.
Tel: 023 8028 3349; www. aabikehirenewforest.co.uk

Country Lanes Cycle Centre
The Railway Station, Brockenhurst.
Tel: 01590 622627;
www.countrylanes.co.uk

Cycle Xperience Bike Hire
Island Shop, 2–4 Brookly Road, Brockenhurst.
Tel: 01590 624204;
www.cyclex.co.uk

Forest Leisure Cycling (FLC)
Burley.
Tel: 01425 403584;
www.forestleisurecycling.co.uk

FISHING

Orchard Lakes
New Lane Orchard, New Lane, Bashley, New Milton.
Tel: 01425 612404
Carp, tench, chub, bream, roach and rudd.

Everton Grange Lake
Braxton Farm, Lymore Lane, Milford on Sea, Lymington.
Tel: 01590 644499
Carp, chub and tench.

RIDING

Burley-Villa School of Riding
Bashley Common Road, New Milton.
Tel: 01425 610278;
www.burleyvilla.co.uk

WALKING

Avon Valley Path
A 34-mile (51km) path from Christchurch to Salisbury Cathedral.

Castleman Trailway
A 16-mile (24km) trail between Upton and Ringwood.

ANNUAL EVENTS & CUSTOMS

Beaulieu
Boat Jumble, Apr.
Auto Jumble, Sep.
Fireworks, end Oct.

Brockenhurst
New Forest Show, last week Jul at New Park.
www.newforestshow.co.uk

Mudeford
Lifeboat Funday, end Jul on Mudeford Quay.

KING WILLIAM
THE SECOND,
SURNAMED RUFUS
BEING SLAIN,
AS BEFORE RELATED,
WAS LAID IN A
CART, BELONGING
TO ONE PURKIS,
AND DRAWN FROM
HENCE, TO
WINCHESTER, AND
BURIED IN THE
CATHEDRAL CHURCH,
OF THAT CITY.

Tea Rooms

The Buttery

19–20 High Street,
Lymington, SO41 9AD
Tel: 01590 672870;
www.thebuttery.org

A well-established and deservedly popular restaurant and tea room, the Buttery serves speciality coffees and teas, clotted cream teas, and a great selection of tasty cakes – all handmade on the premises. You can also get light lunches here, and even a full English breakfast.

The Buttery at the Brock & Bruin

25 Brookley Road,
Brockenhurst, SO42 7RB
Tel: 01590 622958

Home-made cakes and cream teas are top treats at this restaurant and tea room. Light lunches are also served daily, and breakfast too – handy if you're camping.

Montagu Arms Hotel

Palace Lane, Beaulieu,
SO42 7ZL
Tel: 01590 612324; www.montaguarmshotel.co.uk

An hospitable, 16th-century inn nestling in the pretty hamlet of Beaulieu, the Montagu Arms offers finger sandwiches, loaf cakes, scones, cream tea fancies, and shortbread. In season, you can enjoy locally grown strawberries served with your afternoon tea.

Tasty Pastries Bakery and Tea Room

16A High Street, Lyndhurst,
SO43 7BD
Tel: 023 8028 3448

The perfect place to pause for tea and cakes, or perhaps to buy freshly baked pasties, filled baguettes and sandwiches for a picnic.

Pubs

The East End Arms

Main Road, East End,
near Lymington, SO41 5SY
Tel: 01590 626223;
www.eastendarms.co.uk

A traditional New Forest pub serving brasserie-style food in the lounge bar, such as Toulouse sausages and toasted goats' cheese baguettes. No food served Monday, or Sunday evening, or early March and October.

The Filly Inn

Lymington Road, Setley,
Brockenhurst, SO42 7UF
Tel: 01590 623449;
www.fillyinn.co.uk

The bar snacks at this cosy, traditional pub include baguettes and jacket potatoes, and there is a wider menu offering home-baked pies and perhaps roast ribs in barbecue sauce. There is also an extensive Hindi vegetarian menu, and cream teas are offered in summer. Children are welcome, and dogs permitted too.

The Master Builders House Hotel

Bucklers Hard, SO42 7XB
Tel: 01590 616297;
www.themasterbuilders.co.uk

Grassy areas in front of the pub run down to the Beaulieu River, making it a popular spot, especially on summer days. Fish pie and beef bourguignon may appear on the menu, with a good range of light snacks. Beers include Greene King IPA.

The Rose & Thistle

Rockbourne, SP6 3NL
Tel: 01725 518236;
www.roseandthistle.co.uk

This postcard-perfect thatched and whitewashed pub has a rose arch and flowers blooming around the door. Fresh food is cooked to order, from Welsh rarebit and roast beef ploughman's to smoked salmon tagliatelle. There is more substantial fare on the evening menu, such as venison steak with chestnut sauce. Beers include Adnams Broadside and Wadworth 6X.

Isle of Wight

ALUM BAY ■ BEMBRIDGE ■ BRADING ■ CALBOURNE

CARISBROOKE ■ COWES ■ FRESHWATER ■ GODSHILL

NEWPORT ■ NEWTOWN ■ OSBORNE HOUSE ■ CYCLE RIDE 3

RYDE ■ SANDOWN & SHANKLIN ■ SEAVIEW ■ VENTNOR

YARMOUTH ■ WALK 6

■ RYDE

BRADING
BULL RING

...d for baiting Bulls
...om The Middle Ages
Until 1820.

INTRODUCTION

The Isle of Wight is the largest island off England's coast. It is separated from the mainland by the Solent and for many years was isolated and forgotten, until popularised in the mid-19th century by the arrival of Queen Victoria and Prince Albert, who built Osborne House here. This is an island of contrasts: the north facing the mainland; the southwest, including the famous Needles battered by Channel storms; and the southeast basking in a subtropical climate. The Isle of Wight has a timeless, old fashioned appeal which lingers on, born of its long separation from the mainland and an independent way of life; indefinable but nevertheless real, it helps to explain the island's perennial popularity.

6 Walk start point

3 Cycle start point

Fishbourne
Ryde
A3054
Seaview
B3330
Havenstreet
A3055
St Helens
Brading
Bembridge Foreland
B3395
Culver Cliff
Apse
Heath
Sandown
Bay
Sandown
Shanklin
Dunnose
Ventnor

Gosport
Portsmouth
Gilkicker Point

VENTNOR

Unmissable attractions

Join the thousands of boat enthusiasts at Cowes during the island's world-famous sailing regatta held in August...photograph Godshill's chocolate-box pretty, stone and thatched cottages...walk the 15th-century ramparts of Carisbrooke Castle...soak up the atmosphere at stunning Osborne House, Queen Victoria's favourite residence and place of her death...enjoy the traditional seaside amusements and attractions at Sandown...admire the bay views and the quintessentially English beach huts that stand guard on the beach at Shanklin...go to Ventnor, famous in the 19th-century for its alleged curative waters...visit 13th-century Calbourne Mill, still in use today.

1

2

1 Cowes
The town is the scene of the annual Cowes Week regatta when the marina bustles with yachts, sailors and sightseers.

2 Carisbrooke Castle
This 11th-century castle has had a long and varied history but is most well known as a place of imprisonment for Charles I.

3 Freshwater Bay
Popular with walkers, the cove here was well known to Alfred, Lord Tennyson, whose house above the cliffs looked out to sea.

4 Shanklin Chine
Shanklin is home to more than 150 varieties of plants. You will see many of them on a walk through the chine.

5 The Needles
On the hill above the Needles is the 19th-century Needles Battery. The battery formed a part of the coastal defences during both world wars.

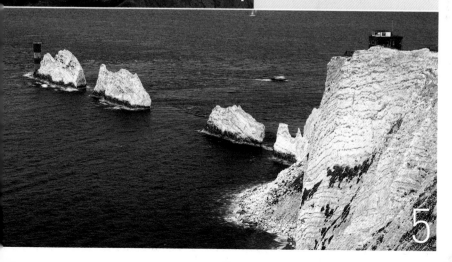

ALUM BAY MAP REF SZ3185

The soaring, spikey chalk outcrops of the Needles are the Isle of Wight's most famous landmark, stretching out to the west and clearly visible from the Dorset coast. Standing around 500 feet (150m) high, they sport a red-and-white striped lighthouse, topped by a small helicopter landing platform, which is best seen via boat trips from Alum Bay.

Set at right angles to the chalk, the cliffs at Alum Bay produce the island's most unusual souvenirs: a range of clear glass novelty items that display the distinctive 12 shades of sand. The colours range from pink and gold to orange and brown, and are all found naturally in the cliffs here. If you're feeling artistic, you can even design your own memento at the Alum Bay Sand Shop, within the Needles Park complex.

The sandstone strata of the cliffs are vertical, and were formed some 50 million years ago. You can view them from a spectacular chairlift ride down the cliffs to the beach at the bottom.

■ Activity

THE TENNYSON TRAIL

This 14-mile (21km) trail starts from Carisbrooke and heads southwest up on to Bowcombe Down, then west past many prehistoric tumuli, and into Brighstone Forest, with views over Brighstone Bay. It then heads back up and over onto Mottistone Down and Brook Down before a long descent past the golf course on Afton Down into Freshwater Bay, where it follows the coast path above the cliff. This is Tennyson Down, with a 38-foot (11.5m) monument to the poet at the high point. The path then drops into Alum Bay.

On the cliff edge is a monument to the noted Italian physicist and inventor, Marconi, who set up a pioneering wireless and telegraph station here at the end of the 19th century.

The Needles Old Battery at Totland is a gun battery and fort with wonderful views over the Needles to the Dorset coast. It was built in 1863 as part of the defences for the large naval base at Portsmouth. Exhibitions tell the story of the fort during the two world wars, and the headland's past as a secret base for rocket testing. Note that access is on foot, and it's a 15-minute walk across the downs from the Alum Bay car park.

BEMBRIDGE MAP REF SZ6588

Bembridge, on the island's eastern tip, was a remote little fishing village in a sheltered haven leading to Brading Quay until the Brading Harbour Improvement and Railway Company set out to reclaim the upper reaches of the haven. They created a deep-water port here, building an embankment between Bembridge and St Helens in 1878 to carry both road and rail. But Bembridge's days as a port were already numbered, and the ferry service to the mainland lasted only until 1888, because the new harbour suffered from silting, although the railway survived until the 20th century.

Today Bembridge is a popular sailing centre and a quiet resort with pleasant walks inland over the reclaimed haven, now marshy meadows, to Brading. At Bembridge Point is the famous Pilot Boat Inn, built in the shape of a boat, and the lifeboat station near by houses displays on its modern, unsinkable craft.

Bembridge Down is crowned by Fort Bembridge (1862–67), the main Victorian fort for the southern Isle of Wight, and offshore, four forts are still visible – the remains of the Victorian defences for Spithead. Bembridge Windmill, half a mile (1km) to the south, dates from 1700 and has its original wooden machinery.

BRADING MAP REF SZ6187

In Roman times Bembridge Down was a separate island and Brading faced it across a tidal channel. In about AD 300 the Romans built a villa here, one of the best in Britain with fabulous mosaics, and it remained occupied until the 5th century. Nowadays a vineyard clothes the slopes near the villa, continuing a tradition begun in Roman times. In 1338 an embankment was built at Yar Bridge, creating a harbour in order to connect Bembridge Down with the rest of the Isle of Wight. Brading became an important port, but the harbour here, too, suffered from increased silting. It was reclaimed in 1878–80 and is now an area of marshy meadows, a favourite breeding ground for birds.

The town's 'Brading the Experience' illustrates in waxworks the famous and infamous characters who populated 2,000 years of Isle of Wight history, as well as displays of wax animals, a fine collection of steam and vintage cars, and a colourful, carousel-themed café. Brading also has the Lilliput Museum of Antique Dolls and Toys. Morton Manor, rebuilt in 1680, claims to possess the island's most beautiful gardens and has a small vineyard producing a range of the island's best wines. The Church of

St Mary, the oldest church on the island, is believed to mark the spot where St Wilfred converted the Isle of Wight to Christianity, and a chapel contains tombs of the Oglander family, important in affairs of the island for 800 years.

To the northwest of Brading is Nunwell House, a 17th-century mansion and seat of the Oglanders from the Norman conquest till 1980. Charles I spent his last night on the island here.

CALBOURNE MAP REF SZ4287

Calbourne is tucked under the downs in the west of the island, an unspoiled little place with a village green, a Norman and a 13th-century church, and pretty stone cottages. The best of these are in Barrington Row, and these low thatched cottages at the back of the village face the diminutive Caul Burn. The stream once powered five watermills. The last surviving, Calbourne Mill, first mentioned in 1299, is still in working order, and there is an attached rural life museum interesting old appliances. West of Calbourne, Chessell Pottery is housed in a large old barn. To the east is historic Swainstone House, now a hotel, renovated after being burnt out in an air raid in 1941. It was named after Swein, the 8th- to 9th-century Danish leader, and later belonged to the Bishop of Winchester. The attached 13th-century chapel survived intact.

To the south of Calbourne, Mottistone Manor Garden has splendid views, and is known for its herbaceous borders and grassy terraces, planted with fruit trees. There are lots of walking trails through the surrounding estate.

CARISBROOKE MAP REF SZ4888

Carisbrooke, once the capital of the Isle of Wight, is inland above the Medina River to the west of the modern capital, Newport, and is overlooked by its castle, one of England's most impressive. High Street is pleasant, and narrow Castle Street leads up from an old ford and a streamside footpath to get to the castle. St Mary's Church, with its lofty 15th-century tower, was the church of a priory dissolved as long ago as 1415.

Carisbrooke Castle is a big, well-preserved Norman fortress built high on an artificial mound. The oldest parts are the keep and the surviving sections of curtain walls, which were constructed in the 12th century and strengthened at the end of the 16th century. A head for heights is needed to walk the ramparts, but you will be rewarded with excellent views of the interior of the castle and the surrounding countryside. A great attraction is the well, 161 feet (49m) deep, with a 16th-century wheel to draw up the water in buckets. It is worked today by donkeys – learn more at the Donkey Centre. The castle also houses the fascinating Isle of Wight Museum.

COWES MAP REF SZ4996

Cowes, on the island's northern tip, is divided by the River Medina. On the west bank is the sailing capital of Britain, on the east is a residential and industrial area, where high-speed ships, flying boats and seaplanes were built during World War II, and the Hovercraft was developed. Beyond all this lies the tranquillity of Osborne House, Queen Victoria's favourite residence.

West Cowes, home of the Royal Yacht Squadron, has an attractive winding High Street and a good array of shops. You can see ships and boats of all sorts from the Victoria Parade. The inaugural Cowes Regatta took place between naval vessels in 1776, and the yacht club was founded in 1815. In 1856 Cowes Castle became the Squadron's headquarters, and the 22 brass guns from the *Royal Adelaide*, King William IV's yacht, were positioned in front of the castle to start races and salute victorious yachts – as they still do. There have always been Royal yachtsmen – including Edward VII, George IV, George V, Prince Philip and Prince Edward – and during Cowes Week in August the little town is alive with the great and the good of the yachting fraternity.

Cowes has a Maritime Museum, a military history museum, and the Sir Max Aitken Museum, which has a display of nautical instruments, paintings and artefacts.

FRESHWATER MAP REF SZ3487

The southwest tip of the Isle of Wight which ends in the jagged sea-girt chalk pinnacles of The Needles is known as the Freshwater Peninsula. The village of Freshwater itself is large and bustling, and was made famous by poet Alfred, Lord Tennyson who came to reside at Farringford – now a hotel – in 1853, soon after he was proclaimed Poet Laureate. He lived there until 1867 when inquisitive visitors, wishing to see the famous man as he walked on the down in cloak and broad-brimmed hat, drove him to his refuge on the Surrey/Sussex border.

Insight

RUINED SHELL

Appuldurcombe House, once Hampshire's finest English baroque building, is now a ruined shell, standing in wooded country to the south amid beautiful grounds landscaped by 'Capability' Brown. The mansion was built in 1710 for Sir Robert Worsley, who is commemorated with an obelisk on the nearby down. The house has been uninhabitable since it was bombed, in 1943, during World War II.

Freshwater has now spread south down the western Yar valley towards Freshwater Bay. The famous portrait photographer Julia Margaret Cameron settled here in the 1860s, and her home, Dimbola Lodge, on Terrace Lane, is now a museum to her work.

GODSHILL MAP REF SZ5383

Nestling prettily beneath its beautiful 15th-century church tower, this little village of stone-built, thatched cottages is the most visited and photographed place on the island. Attractions include the interesting model of Godshill village and the Nostalgia Toy Museum, and the Old Smithy and Gardens. Godshill is very popular, so come early in the morning to avoid the coaches and the crowds or in the evening after they have gone.

However, one peaceful haven here is the lovely church, which is almost 1,000 years old and contains a rare medieval wall painting, a painting of Daniel in the lions' den (attributed to Rubens), and some monuments to the Worsley family of Appuldurcombe. The nearby Owl and Falconry Centre offers flying displays.

NEWPORT MAP REF SZ5088

Newport, the capital of the Isle of Wight, is a venerable old market town on the River Medina. Its squares and narrow, twisting streets may hide the river from the view of the cursory visitor but boats still ply their trade at the rejuvenated quay. Here, too, you'll find the arts centre, housed in a large converted warehouse. The pleasant High Street has many attractive buildings, and is dominated by the Guildhall, with its fine Ionic portico market designed by John Nash, now home to the Museum of Island History. St Thomas' Church has a beautiful marble monument designed by Marochetti to Princess Elizabeth, the youngest daughter of Charles I, who died of a fever aged 14 while she was a prisoner in Carisbrooke Castle.

The town was founded in medieval times as the 'new port' for the old capital, Carisbrooke, yet, similarly to Carisbrooke, it can claim to have its roots in Roman times, since a Roman villa, dating from the 3rd century AD, was discovered here in 1926. The villa has been excavated and is now open to the public. Three of the public rooms have tessellated floors, and the largest also has a fireplace – this was an unusual feature in a Roman house. There is also a reconstructed Roman herb garden.

Just to the northwest of the town is Parkhurst Prison and further on you'll find Parkhurst Forest, the remaining glades and woodlands of a former royal hunting forest. This ancient woodland has been threaded by waymarked paths and is now one of the last remaining refuges of the red squirrel.

NEWTOWN MAP REF SZ4291

Newtown was originally founded in the 13th century on the island's northwest coast, and its grid-iron pattern can be recognised even today. Its large natural harbour was reputed to have anchorage for 50 ships, but continual silting reduced its size and this, coupled with raids by the French, led to the town's decline. Today the little 17th-century Town Hall is in the care of the National Trust, and the harbour is now a nature reserve, echoing to the piping of the curlew and the harsh cry of wild geese.

At the head of one of the creeks is Shalfleet, where you can explore the old harbour on foot, heading down to the quay which is now busy with pleasure craft. Shalfleet's Church of St Michael was saved in a small-scale replay of the saving of Winchester Cathedral. When its stout Norman tower was found to be standing in 10 feet (3m) of clay and water and in danger of collapsing, the foundations were relaid in concrete.

OSBORNE HOUSE

MAP REF SZ5296

Osborne House, overlooking the Solent to the east of Cowes, was designed as a royal country retreat by Prince Albert and Thomas Cubitt in the fashionable style of a Neapolitan villa, complete with stylish Italianate campaniles and a loggia. Started in 1845, it served both as a family home and for state functions, and this duality is reflected in the mix of homely and grand interiors on display today. Private rooms include the sitting room where the Queen and her consort worked together. Grander, state rooms include the Durbar Room, which has an Indian-style plasterwork ceiling, where a selection of Indian gifts presented to Victoria, Empress of India, are displayed.

Outside are terraced gardens and a walled fruit and flower garden. In the grounds is the lovely Swiss Cottage, a child-size royal playhouse, charmingly furnished in miniature. The playhouse had a serious purpose, too: the royal princes learned about carpentry here, the princesses learned how to cook and manage a household, and each child had a garden plot in which to grow some vegetables and flowers. A museum next door shows mementoes collected by the Queen's children and grandchildren.

Victoria and Albert loved to walk in the woods at Osborne, and the Prince added to these extensively, planting every sort of British tree. The Queen recorded lovingly in her memoirs that nightingales were frequently to be heard.

Queen Victoria died at Osborne House, in 1901, and her successor Edward VII presented the well-loved mansion to the nation.

Nearby Barton is a much older place, with a medieval manor house rebuilt by Prince Albert as an experimental farm. Today its gardens are open to the public, along with an award-winning vineyard.

■ Insight

OSBORNE HOUSE

During World War I, Osborne House became a convalescent home for officers. Among the men who came here were A A Milne, (creator of *Winnie the Pooh*), and Robert Graves, who recalled staying here in his memoir, *Goodbye to All That* (1929).

A linear ride from Cowes to Newport

This ride makes a relaxed day out, with easy access from the mainland. There is a lot to see from the safe, level trail, which follows the National Cycle Network route along the former Cowes-to-Newport railway line. Route-finding is straightforward, and you'll enjoy some lovely views across the River Medina, with plenty of opportunities for birdwatching on the way.

Route Directions

1 From Medina Road turn into Bridge Road, signposted 'Newport via cycleway'. Follow the road to the mini-roundabout at the top of the hill and turn left into Arctic Road, still following the signposted cycle route. Pass the UK Sailing Academy on your left and continue to the very end of the road.

2 Zig-zag right and left as the cycle route joins the old railway line, which edges its way clear of industrial Cowes through a tunnel of trees. Pass the signposted footpath to Northwood on your right and, a little further on, look out for the broken remains of an old iron and timber bridge.

3 Beyond the bridge, look out for a distinctive tall spire and pinnacles above the trees across the river. Around half a mile (800m) from the gates of Osborne House, St Mildred's church at Whippingham was remodelled in the mid-18th century for use by the royal family. Continue straight on along the track.

4 Now the views start to really open up, and between Pinkmead and Stag Lane you'll spot the old Ryde paddle steamer slowly rusting in her mud berth at Island

Harbour Marina on the opposite bank. The hedges are thick with blackthorn, dog rose and crab apple, and in summer you'll see red admiral butterflies and dragonflies. Listen, too, for the plaintive call of curlews.

5 Now the trail crosses the old trestle viaduct that once carried the railway line over Dodnor Creek. This area of open water, marshland and woodland was created in the 1790s when the creek was dammed to provide power for a proposed tide mill. Today the creek is a local nature reserve and you may see reed warblers, coots, moorhens and grey herons. Beyond the creek the cycleway climbs briefly across Dodnor Lane and approaches industrial buildings on the edge of Newport. Look out for a pair of concrete tracks that cross the trail and lead to a pair of slim concrete jetties built out into the river. A rolling gantry loads industrial products onto waiting barges. The facility was specially designed to minimise disturbance to the birds feeding on the mudflats of this protected wildlife site. Soon, reach the white gate at the end of the traffic-free route. Continue straight ahead as far as the post-box

Route facts

DISTANCE/TIME 8 miles (12.9km) 1h45

MAP OS OS Explorer OL29 Isle of Wight

START Medina Road pay-and-display car park, West Cowes, grid ref: SZ 499956

TRACKS Back streets of Cowes, tarred and level cycle track

GETTING TO THE START Take the A3020 from Newport to West Cowes and follow signs to the floating bridge. Passengers arriving with their bikes on the car ferry should follow the one-way system to the right, and cross the floating bridge to begin the ride in Medina Road, West Cowes.

CYCLE HIRE Funation Cycle Hire, Cowes. Tel: 01983 200300; www.funation.co.uk

THE PUB The Bargeman's Rest, Newport. Tel: 01983 525828; www.bargemansrest.com

❶ A short hill to begin and two sections of road. Ideal for beginners and children aged eight and over.

on the corner of Hurstake Road. Turn left to The Bargeman's Rest, and bear right at the bottom of the hill for the final 300yds (274m) to the pub.

6 Take a break before retracing your route to Cowes.

RYDE MAP REF 5993

When island visitors disembark at Ryde from the Portsmouth ferry, ex-London Transport underground trains take them down the 0.5-mile (800m) long pier, necessary because the coast shelves so gently that vessels can get no closer.

Ryde was developed in the late 18th century and is the largest town on the island, with some 24,000 residents. It has the usual seaside amusements as well as 5-mile (8km) long sandy beach. From the promenade there are superb views across Spithead and three of the Solent's Victorian forts. Ryde's summer carnival is a spectacular event.

Southwest of Ryde is Brickfields Horse Country, with horses of all sizes, wagon rides and pig-racing. At Ashey, Rosemary Vineyard, the largest of the island's three vineyards, offers tours, tastings and a shop. At Fishbourne, to the west, is Quarr Abbey, a modern foundation (1907–14) of Benedictine monks near the ruins of the earlier Cistercian Abbey. The Isle of Wight Steam Railway puffs out of Smallbrook Junction, just south of Ryde on its journey past Havenstreet to Wootton.

SANDOWN & SHANKLIN
MAP REF SZ5984

The honky-tonk seaside neighbour of more sedate Shanklin, Sandown was founded as a resort in about 1800 and faces southeastwards out to sea across Sandown Bay. It is built at beach level, with the immense chalk walls of Culver Cliff to the north and the cliffed coast of Shanklin and Luccombe to the south. Sandown is a popular venue for family holidays, with its 6 miles (9.6km) of sandy beach and an esplanade and amusement park, a pier of 1878, cinema, zoo specialising in tigers and lemurs, and the fascinating Dinosaur Isle, a museum displaying life-size dinosaurs and offering guided fossil walks. At the Garlic Farm, near Newchurch, you can buy and learn more.

Shanklin, the quieter neighbour to the south, is a resort that developed with the coming of the railway in 1891, and now has the best collection of beach huts on the island. You reach the beach by a lift from the clifftop, which has a superb view around Sandown Bay to the gleaming white heights of Culver Cliff. Inland is Shanklin Old Village, a former fishing village close to the winding glen of Shanklin Chine. This 300-feet (91.5m) deep, wooded and ferny fissure was much beloved of earlier tourists, including the poet, John Keats, who stayed at the Old Village in 1819 and composed part of 'Endymion' here. The Victorians flocked to tread its winding path past the 40-foot (12m) waterfall to the beach. Today, Shanklin Chine still pulls the crowds – its rare flora is of great interest – and the resort also has two theatres and seaside amusements.

SEAVIEW MAP REF SZ6392

This family holiday resort to the east of Ryde is renowned for its gently sloping, firm, sandy beach, from which there is safe bathing. The town still basks in 19th-century charm, with narrow streets lined with villas and shops sloping down to the sea, the peace maintained by the lack of a main through road. Saltern

Cottages are a reminder of the old salt industry which thrived here on the bleak marshes in the days before Seaview became a select resort for those who shun the bustle and gaiety of Ryde. To the northwest is the famous Seaview Wildlife Encounter (formerly Flamingo Park), a bird sanctuary where flamingos, peacocks and waterfowl wander freely over green lawns.

VENTNOR MAP REF SZ5777

This south coast resort climbs the sheer cliff beneath flat St Boniface Down (the highest point on the island), as a series of terraces behind the sandy beach, so that the mainly Victorian buildings are built-up in layers and are joined by steep zig-zagging roads with corkscrew turns. There is something Mediterranean in this arrangement, and Ventnor has been dubbed 'the English Madeira'. Also, the climate, too, is very good. Protected by the bulk of St Boniface Down, it basks in subtropical conditions.

Ventnor was a small fishing village up until 1841 – albeit much involved in smuggling – but in that year, a famous doctor, Sir James Clarke, publicly sang its praises and visitors started to come. The railway arrived in 1866, meaning Ventnor's development as a health resort was assured, attracting, among others, authors Macaulay, Dickens and Thackeray. Later it was the site of the Royal National Hospital for Consumption and Diseases of the Chest. The town's history is explained in Ventnor's Heritage Museum which has an extensive archive.

Ventnor divides into two parts, the elegant 'town' on the cliff face, where

■ Visit

THE AUSTRALIAN CONNECTION

In the days when convicts were transported to Australia, most of them left Britain from ships moored off Ryde – the last they ever saw of 'the old country'. Because of this there remains a special connection between the town and Australia. St Thomas' Church is now a heritage centre with an exhibition commemorating the first ships that carried prisoners to Australia, as well as displays of other local history.

■ Insight

THE LOSS OF THE *EURIDICE*

In 1878 a fine, fully rigged sailing frigate sank off Dunnose Head, south of Shanklin, with the loss of 300 souls. The *Euridice* was a Royal Navy training ship, on her way to Bermuda with a full complement of passengers and crew. It was March and the weather was terrible, but sheltered in the lee of the cliffs, the ship sailed on in ignorance of the true conditions, its portholes open to ventilate the two decks. As she rounded the point and the true storm hit, she took on water and sank in the freezing waters.

■ Insight

OLD MONEY

According to local history, Yarmouth man and hero Robert Holmes (1622–1692) sailed with the King's fleet to Guinea off the west coast of Africa. During this service Holmes' ship took aggressive action against a vessel that belonged to the Dutch West India Company which resulted in a large amount of Dutch gold allegedly being shipped back to England by Holmes. This gold was then melted down and made into coins – known as 'guineas'.

YARMOUTH

Ventnor ales are still brewed, and the seaside resort at the foot of the cliff. The extraordinary climate is manifest in the Ventnor Botanic Gardens, planted in the 1970s, where some 3,500 species include palms and cork trees. The interesting Smuggling Museum, hidden in subterranean caverns beneath the Botanic Garden, has a large collection of fascinating relics, vividly illustrating the days when Ventnor was the unofficial 'headquarters' of illicit trade. Near by is the ancient village of St Lawrence with the Rare Breeds and Waterfowl Park. Isle of Wight Glass, founded in 1973, produces an exciting range of award-winning glassware.

The southern coast between Ventnor and St Catherine's Point is a region of landslides, where great masses of sandstone rock have been, and continue to be, carried down into the sea on a lubricating layer of blue clay. In fact, Ventnor has the biggest urban landslide problem in Britain. The Undercliff, a ledge which extends along the cliffs, is actually the top of an ancient landslide block. To appreciate the coast to the full, walk part of the coastal path between Shanklin and Blackgang. From Shanklin the path first lies close to, and then on, the shore until Ventnor and beyond. At St Lawrence, the path climbs up beyond the road and affords good views to the south before you reach Blackgang.

Nearby Blackgang Chine is an extraordinary theme park that combines static displays with fast fairground rides and lovely gardens. In fact the gardens were the initial inspiration for the park, created to attract Victorian vacationers.

YARMOUTH MAP REF SZ3689

The Lymington–Yarmouth ferry is the picturesque way of entry to the Isle of Wight, for Yarmouth is a compact little town with narrow streets and attractive houses, and a small harbour busy with yachts and a flourishing boatbuilder's yard. During the Middle Ages it was the most important Isle of Wight town, but decline set in and by 1800 it had only a few hundred inhabitants.

Yarmouth's sturdy castle was built against the French in 1547 by Henry VIII, and it remained in use until the 1870s. It is hidden down an alley by the ferry, on King's Land, and is easy to miss. The pier near the lifeboat station was built in 1876 and was originally the landing stage for the Lymington ferry, but now it is a pleasant walkway.

Yarmouth's church, rebuilt 1614–26, contains an intriguing monument to Sir Robert Holmes, Governor of the Isle of Wight during the reign of Charles II. The figure was originally intended as a statue of the French 'Sun King', Louis XIV. The statue was being transported by sea so that the sculptor could complete the head from life, but Holmes captured the ship carrying it, took the statue and had his own likeness attached to it instead. Holmes entertained Charles II at his house on the quay in Yarmouth, now the George Hotel.

West of Yarmouth is Fort Victoria Country Park, based around the remains of a fort built in 1855. The many parts of the park afford superb views of the Solent, and there are guided walks, an interesting maritime heritage exhibition, a marine aquarium and planetarium.

From Yarmouth to Freshwater

West Wight is a peaceful area of great natural beauty, offering swathes of open countryside, cliffs, wonderful views and fascinating wildlife. This three-part ramble encapsulates the contrasting landscapes of the area, from the wildlife-rich tidal estuary of the River Yar and the wetland habitat of freshwater marshes that are home to many species of wild birds, to rolling farmland and the magnificent chalk headlands and hills with their breathtaking coastal views.

Route Directions

1 From the car park go to the town square. Head for the church and walk along St James' Street. Cross Tennyson Road into Mill Road and carry on until you pass the old Tide Mill. Continue through the gate and turn right on the old railway line, following it for about 1.5 miles (2.4 km) to The Causeway.

2 For the short walk back to Yarmouth, turn right, cross The Causeway to The Red Lion and Point 9. For the second stage of the walk, turn left at Point 2 and follow the lane to the B3399. Turn left and cross into the unsurfaced Manor Road. In 50yds (46m) bear left – 'Freshwater Way' – and ascend towards Afton Down.

3 Proceed ahead at a junction beside the golf course, and follow the gravel track to the clubhouse. Go through a gate and walk down the access track, keeping left to reach the A3055. Turn right downhill into Freshwater Bay.

4 For the second loop option, walk past the Albion Hotel and continue, turning right at Blackbridge Road, at Point 8. For the third section of the long walk, turn left instead by the bus shelter and toilets, along a metalled track, the 'Coastal Footpath'. As it bears left, keep ahead through kissing gates and steeply ascend a concrete path on to Tennyson Down. Keep to the well trodden path to reach the memorial cross at the top.

5 Continue down the wide grassy swathe to reach the replica of Old Nodes Beacon. Here, turn very sharp right down a chalk track. Turn right into a car park and almost immediately climb sharp left.

6 The path drops to a gate. Proceed along the woodland fringe into a more open area, then fork left at disused excavations on the right. Cross a stile, then keep left and after 50yds (46m) turn sharp left and descend to

another stile. Cross the next field to a stile and turn right along the field edge to a stile.

7 After the next stile cross a farm track, go through a gate and walk along the track (F47) beside Farringford Manor Hotel. Pass beneath a wooden footbridge and continue down to a gate and the road. Turn right, pass the thatched church, and turn left down Blackbridge Road.

8 Just before Black Bridge, turn left into Afton Marshes Nature Reserve. Walk along the nature trail, cross over the footbridge and then turn left following the path beside the stream (this can be very wet) to the A3055. Turn left and almost immediately cross over to join footpath F61 along the course of the old railway. After 0.5 mile (800m) reach The Causeway.

9 Turn left and follow the lane to All Saints Church and The Red Lion pub. Take the path

Route facts

DISTANCE/TIME
9.5 miles (15.3km) 4h30

MAP OS Outdoor Leisure 29
Isle of Wight

START Ferry terminal or
pay-and-display car park
opposite, Yarmouth,
grid ref: SZ 354897

TRACKS Disused railway,
woodland and downland
paths, some road walking,
4 stiles

GETTING TO THE START
Yarmouth is 10 miles
(16.1km) west of Newport
on the A3054. The car park
is opposite the ferry
terminal. Alternatively,
park at the ferry terminal
in Lymington and cross
to Yarmouth as a foot
passenger on the Wightlink
ferry (www.wightlink.co.uk).

THE PUB The Red Lion,
Church Place, Freshwater.
Tel: 01983 754925;
www.redlion-wight.co.uk

(Freshwater Way F1) between
a cottage and the churchyard
wall. Cross two stiles and
continue along the farm road.
At the farmyard entrance
cross the double stile on the
left and bear right along the
field edge to a stile.

10 When you reach a track
and the entrance to Kings
Manor Farm, cross the stile
ahead and follow the wide
track to a gate and a junction.
Climb the stile on the right,
pass through a copse, over
another stile and bear left,
uphill along the field edge.
Cross a stile and head to
another stile. Descend into
woodland, emerging onto a
metalled track. Turn left to
the A3054 and right to the
bridge over the river, back
into Yarmouth.

◼ TOURIST INFORMATION CENTRES

Cowes
The Arcade, Fountain Quay.
Tel: 01983 813818

Newport
The Guildhall, High Street.
Tel: 01983 813818

Ryde
Western Esplanade.
Tel: 01983 813818

Sandown
8 High Street.
Tel: 01983 813818

Shanklin
67 High Street.
Tel: 01983 813818

Yarmouth
The Quay.
Tel: 01983 813818

◼ PLACES OF INTEREST

Adgestone Vinyard
Brading.
Tel: 01983 402503;
www.adgestonevineyard.co.uk

Appuldurcombe House
Godshill.
Tel: 01983 852484;
www.english-heritage.org.uk

Barton Manor Gardens & Vineyard
East Cowes.
Tel: 01983 292835

Bembridge Windmill (NT)
High Street, Bembridge.
Tel: 01983 873945;

Brading Roman Villa
Brading.
Tel: 01983 406223;
www.bradingromanvilla.org.uk

Calbourne Water Mill
Tel: 01983 531227;
www.calbournewatermill.co.uk

Carisbrooke Castle & Isle of Wight Museum (EH)
1.5 miles (2km) southeast of Newport.
Tel: 01983 522107

Fort Victoria Country Park
Near Yarmouth.
Tel: 01983 823893;
www.fortvictoria.co.uk

Heritage Museum
11 Spring Hill, Ventnor.
Tel: 01983 855407;
www.ventnorheritage.org.uk

Isle of Wight Steam Railway
Tel: 01983 884343;
www.iwsteamrailway.co.uk

Maritime Museum
Beckford Road, Cowes.
Tel: 01983 823433

Morton Manor
Brading.
Tel: 01983 406168

Mottistone Manor Garden (NT)
Tel: 01983 741302

Museum of Island History
Guildhall, Newport.
Tel: 01983 823366;
www.iwight.com

The Needles Old Battery (NT)
West Highdown, Totland.
Tel: 01983 754772

The Needles Park
Tel: 0870 458 0022;
www.theneedles.co.uk

Newport Roman Villa
Cypress Road, Newport.
Tel: 01983 529720;
www.romans-in-britain.org.uk

Nostalgia Toy Museum
High Street, Godshill.
Tel: 01983 840181

Osborne House and Gardens (EH)
East Cowes
Tel: 01983 200022

Rosemary Vineyard
Ashey, Ryde.
Tel: 01983 811084;
www.rosemaryvineyard.co.uk

Shanklin Chine
Shanklin.
Tel: 01983 866432;
www.shanklinchine.co.uk

Smuggling Museum
Botanic Garden, Ventnor.
Tel: 01983 853677

Yarmouth Castle (EH)
Yarmouth.
Tel: 01983 760678

◼ FOR CHILDREN

Amazon World Zoo Park
Watery Lane, near Arreton.
Tel: 01983 867122;
www.amazonworld.co.uk

Blackgang Chine
Chale, near Ventnor.
Tel: 01983 730052;
www.blackgangchine.com

Godshill Model Village
Old Vicarage Gardens, Godshill.
Tel: 01983 840270; www.modelvillagegodshill.co.uk

Isle of Wight Owl and Falconry Centre
Appledurcombe.
Tel: 01983 852484;
www.appledurcombe.co.uk

Isle of Wight Zoo
Yaverland Seafront, Sandown.
Tel: 01983 403883;
www.isleofwightzoo.com
Seaview Wildlife Encounter
Tel: 01983 612261;
www.flamingoparkiw.com

▓ SHOPPING

Arreton Barns Craft Village
Main Road, Arreton.
Tel: 01983 539361;
www.arretonbarns.co.uk
Bonchurch Pottery
Shore Road, Bonchurch.
Tel: 01983 854445
The Cider Barn
High Street, Godshill.
Tel: 01983 840680
**Isle of Wight Farmers'
Market**
St Thomas' Square, Newport.
Every Fri.

▓ PERFORMING ARTS

Medina Theatre
Fairlee Road, Newport.
Tel: 01983 527020
Ryde Theatre
Lind Street, Ryde.
Tel: 01983 568 099
Shanklin Theatre
Prospect Road, Shanklin.
Tel: 01983 862739

▓ SPORTS & ACTIVITIES

ADRENALINE SPORTS
**Wight Water Adventure
Watersports**
Tel: 01983 404987;
www.wightwaters.com

**High Adventure
Yarmouth.**
Tel: 07774 614883;
www.islandactivities.co.uk
Paragliding and fast boats.
BOAT TRIPS
Needles Pleasure Cruises
Tel: 01983 761567
CYCLE HIRE
Battersby Cycles
Ryde.
Tel: 01983 562039
Extreme Cycles
Ventnor.
Tel: 01983 852232
Wight Offroad
Tel: 01983 730120;
www.wightoffroad.co.uk
FISHING
**Island Fish Farm and
Meadow Lakes**
Muggleton Lane, near
Brighstone.
Tel: 01983 740941
Scotties Fishing Tackle
11 Lugley Street, Newport.
Tel: 01983 522115;
www.scotties-tackle.co.uk
HORSE-RIDING
Allendale Equestrian Centre
Newport Road, Godshill.
Tel: 01983 840258
Brickfields Horse Country
Binstead, near Ryde.
Tel: 01983 566801;
www.brickfields.net

▓ ANNUAL EVENTS & CUSTOMS

Cowes
Cowes Week; late Jul–early

Aug. Tel: 01983 295744;
www.cowesweek.co.uk
Isle of Wight County Show
Northwood Showground,
mid-Aug. Tel: 01980 813800;
www.riwas.org.uk
Newchurch
Garlic Festival, mid-Aug.
Tel: 01983 863566; www.
garlic-festival.co.uk
Newport
Isle of Wight Festival; pop
festival; mid-Jun.
Tel: 08705 321321;
www.isleofwightfestival.org
Ryde
Carnival, end Aug/early Sep.
Yarmouth
Old Gaffers Festival, gaff-
rigged yachts; early Jun.
Tel: 01983 760541;
www.yarmoutholdgaffersfesti
val.co.uk
Isle of Wight Cycling Festival
Mid-Sep.
Tel: 01983 823355; www.sun
seaandcycling.com
**Isle of Wight Walking
Festival**
Mid-May.
Tel: 01983 203888;
www.isleofwightwalkingfestiv
al.co.uk
Round the Island Race
Early Jun.
Tel: 01983 296911;
www.roundtheisland.org.uk
White Air
Extreme sports festival,
end Oct.
www.whiteair.co.uk

Tea Rooms

Vineyard Café

Adgestone Vineyard, Upper Adgestone Road, Brading, PO36 0ES
Tel: 01983 402503;
www.adgestonevineyard.co.uk

The oldest vineyard in Britain serves some of the best cream teas on the Isle of Wight, with freshly baked scones, and home-made cakes. Morning coffee and light lunches – including wine – are also available, and check ahead for special musical evenings.

God's Providence House

12 St Thomas Square, Newport
Tel: 01983 522085

This is the spot where, it is claimed, the Great Plague of the 1560s came to a halt – hence the name. Today it's a traditional tea room, serving coffee, teas and lunches.

Pearly Boise Ice Cream Parlour

57 High Street, Shanklin
Tel: 01983 864611

This wonderful emporium offers home-made ice cream in 27 flavours, including apple crumble, white choc and orange Cointreau. There are also sorbets to whet your appetite, and traditional milkshakes and sundaes.

And for a retro treat, enjoy a knickerbocker glory! Coffee and pastries are available.

The Old World Tearooms & Gardens

The High Street, Godshill
Tel: 01983 840637

This popular, family-run tea room in the highly photogenic village of Godshill serves delicious cream teas, as well as morning coffee, tasty light lunches, and a good range of sandwiches and baguettes. Eat indoors or out.

Pubs

Buddle Inn

St Catherines Road, Niton
Tel: 01983 730243

This is one of the island's oldest hostelries in a former 16th-century farmhouse. There are stone flags, oak beams and a large open fire inside and dogs and muddy boots are welcome. Home-cooked food includes local crab and lobster, curries, pies and ploughman's, and there's a good choice of wines and real ales.

The Folly

Folly Lane, Cowes.
Tel: 01983 297171

Easy access by both land and water makes this unusual Cowes pub a very popular venue in summer. It was constructed in part from the timbers out of the hull of an old barge, and makes good use of its nautical theme, offering a blackboard menu that includes spicy sausage 'Crewpot' casserole, or maybe fresh fish.

The New Inn

Mill Lane, Shalfleet
Tel: 01983 531314

Beamed ceilings, a flagstone floor and big open fireplaces characterise this fine 18th-century inn on the coastal path route. They specialise in fish and seafood, with unusual offerings such as Cajun-style salmon, and hake with tarragon and lemon, alongside favourites such as duck in orange sauce. There are around 60 wines, plus beers such as Flowers Bitter and Marston's Pedigree.

The Red Lion

Church Place, Freshwater
Tel: 01983 754925

The pub has a pleasant setting on the River Yar. Everything here is freshly made. Favourites might include gammon with parsley sauce, smoked haddock pâté, and apple pie and custard. The garden includes a herb garden – the perfect place to sup a pint of local Goddards ale – and dogs are permitted.

Portsmouth & Southeast Coast

BOTLEY ■ FAREHAM ■ HAMBLE ■ HAYLING ISLAND

WALK 7 ■ NETLEY ■ PORTCHESTER CASTLE ■ PORTSMOUTH

SOUTHAMPTON ■ SOUTHSEA ■ TITCHFIELD ■ WALK 8

The great Hampshire ports, commercial Southampton and naval-fleet based Portsmouth, comprise the largest urban area on England's south coast. During the 20th century they spread, eating up lesser harbours and towns and creeping inland. Among all this are the nature reserves at Langstone Harbour and Titchfield Haven, the popular beaches around Southsea, and the many marinas that line the Solent's shores. Wartime memories abound in this area, too – thousands of men, women and boats congregated here for the invasion of occupied Europe during World War II.

7 Walk start point

Unmissable attractions

Go to the top of Portsmouth's striking Spinnaker Tower for superb views over the British Navy's most important historical base...see the coastal differences by walking part of the Solent Way...spend, spend, spend at Southampton's glossy West Quay shopping centre...witness boat-building at its best on The Hamble...marvel at 3rd-century Roman Portchester Castle...come face to face with a shark at Southsea's fantastic Blue Reef Aquarium...visit writer William Cobbett's beloved Botley.

1

1 Spinnaker Tower
Most people choose to use the lift, rather than Climb the 572 steps to the third-view deck. Apart from the awesome panorama, there is a challenging view down through a glass floor. Do you dare to step onto it?

2 HMS *Victory*
The prow of Admiral Horatio Nelson's flagship HMS *Victory*, has been beautifully restored and can be admired at Portsmouth Maritime Museum.

3 Netley Abbey
Monastic life flourished at the abbey until the Dissolution. The structure was destroyed when it was converted into a home.

BOTLEY MAP REF SU5213

The political writer and champion of the underdog William Cobbett farmed here between 1804 and 1817. He described this attractive redbrick village, where he was actually constantly quarrelling with the local parson, as 'the most delightful village in the world', and he is fondly celebrated with a memorable stone in the village square and a walking trail around the village. Botley remains delightful, its wide main street and busy square dominated by a little porticoed Market Hall of 1848. The mill on the River Hamble, listed in the Domesday Book, is now a crafts centre. Botley was once a small port at the head of the Hamble River.

Just to the south, extensive Manor Farm Country Park, 400 acres (162ha) of varied habitats, supports a range of plants and animals, with riverside and woodland walks. The park's Manor Farm Museum is a traditional farm offering hands-on experience of pigs, cows and other livestock. East of Botley, Wickham Vineyard offers a taste of English wines.

■ Insight

WILLIAM COBBETT

Born in Fareham in 1763, William Cobbett was a self-educated man with forthright views. After fleeing to America to avoid prosecution, he developed his talents as a pamphleteer. He returned to England in 1802 to start a newspaper, travelled and wrote books, including *Rural Rides* (1830), an account of his travels across southern England. He supported the underdog in a pithy and opinionated style, adopting more radical anti-government views. In 1832 he became a Member of Parliament.

FAREHAM MAP REF SU5706

Fareham's attractive old High Street has a complementary mix of architecture – 18th-century brick, Victorian stucco and earlier timber. Since World War II the old town has expanded and now merges with neighbouring parishes in a sprawl of houses and industry. Nevertheless the centre remains appealing, and visitors can appreciate the 19th-century novelist William Thackeray's description of it as a 'dear little old Hampshire town'.

During the Middle Ages Fareham was a major port, until the channels silted up. Prosperity returned in the 18th and 19th centuries with shipbuilding for the navy, and the big, attractive houses on the High Street were built for senior naval men. Today there are high-tech industries as well as an entertainment centre and a shopping mall. Fareham Creek, popular with the yachting fraternity, is now a conservation area.

In 1784 at Funtley, near Fareham, Henry Cort invented a process of creating wrought iron which helped keep Britain's economy together during the Napoleonic Wars. British iron ores are generally low grade, and during the wars, foreign ores could not get through – a potentially disastrous state of affairs affecting the production of horseshoes, tools and nails. Cort devised the method of 'puddling', where the molten metal was stirred with iron bars – a process that separated the ore from impurities and allowed the production of wrought iron. Little remains today of the iron works, but what there is can be seen beside the footpath off the Wickham to Titchfield road beside the M27.

HAMBLE MAP REF SU4807

Once a main site of a flourishing naval dockyard, the village of Hamble and the estuary of the little river that shares its name are still popular with sailors of the small pleasure craft that crowd its busy waters as they sail or motor in and out of Southampton Water. The older parts of the village, unpretentious in brick, go down to the quayside near the jetties, the marina and the boat-building yards.

Hamble was a favoured place of embarkation during the Napoleonic Wars and troops were mustered here. In more recent times Hamble has had strong links with the aircraft industry, with a British Aerospace factory and airfield where airline pilots were trained.

The nearby village of Bursledon has the last steam-driven brickworks in the country, founded in 1897, and Hampshire's only working windmill.

HAYLING ISLAND

MAP REF SU7303

This small, popular island separates the tidal creeks, sprawling mudflats and low-lying saltmarshes of Langstone and Chichester harbours. The northern part is chiefly rural while the southern part, facing over the Channel, has been a resort since the mid-19th century. It has a 5-mile (8km) long sandy beach, select golf club and all the paraphernalia of a holiday resort devoted to water sports, particularly windsurfing. Drivers should note that there is only one road to and from the island, and it can get very busy. The seafront is dominated by the huge Norfolk Crescent, erected in the early 19th century. The 13th-century church at

■ **Insight**

SAILING ON THE SOLENT
The Solent is said to contain the largest pleasure sailing fleet in the world, with more than 32,000 yacht berths in the plethora of marinas along the coast stretching from Southampton Water to Chichester Harbour. The sailing is safe here, in the sheltered lagoons of Portsmouth, Langstone and Chichester harbours, in Southampton Water and in the Solent, where craft are protected from the open Channel by the Isle of Wight. Hamble is the yachting capital of Southampton Water and Ocean Village, in Southampton's old Alexandra Dock, is a superb marina where hundreds of yachts are moored, and there are plenty of shops and restaurants.

South Hayling stands on the island's highest point – the yew tree in the churchyard is a true Saxon, probably 1,000 years old; the Saxon font is one of only a handful of that age in Hampshire.

Sandy Point to the southeast and Langstone Harbour along to the west are designated nature reserves and both are important overwintering grounds for geese and waders. Langstone Harbour is the central of three shallow lagoons and remains a mostly wild, saltmarsh-girt, muddy place. The harbour itself covers some 5,000 acres (2,025ha) and contains a 1,370-acre (555ha) RSPB reserve, at its best in September and through the winter when it is full of migrant waders, including Brent geese, dunlin, turnstones and rare black-tailed godwits. There are frequent sightings of resident oystercatchers, redshanks, herons and shelducks.

A circuit from Hamble to Bursledon

The villages of Hamble and Old Bursledon are a delight to explore. Hamble has a twisting main street, lined with pretty Georgian buildings, leading down to the Quay with lovely river views. Old Bursledon has peaceful lanes dotted with interesting buildings. Tucked away on the slopes above the river, you'll find it a pleasure to stroll through lanes going nowhere, especially if you stop at the Hacketts Marsh viewpoint.

Route Directions

1 From the quayside car park walk to the pontoon and get on the passenger ferry to cross the estuary to Warsash (ferry times, weather permitting, Monday–Friday 7am–5.15pm; Saturday and Sunday 8.30am–6pm). Turn left along the raised gravel path beside the estuary and mudflats. Cross a footbridge and continue straight on until you get to a gravelled parking area. During exceptionally high tides the path may flood so, if this happens, walk through the car park and rejoin the path by the marina.

2 At a boatyard keep right of a boat shed. Bear left beyond, between the shed and TS Marina, and bear right in front of the sales office to rejoin the path. On joining the road, continue straight on between the industrial buildings to the A27.

3 Turn left and then cross Bursledon Bridge. (Turn right before the bridge if you wish to visit the historic Bursledon Brickworks.) Pass beneath the railway and turn left, signed to the station. Turn left into Station Road, then left again into the station car park, following signs for The Jolly Sailor pub. Climb a steep path to the road. Turn left at the junction, then left again to reach the pub.

4 Return along the lane and fork left along the High Street into Old Bursledon. Pause at the bench and viewpoint at Hacketts Marsh, then bear left at the phone-box along the High Street. Pass The Vine Inn and Salterns Lane into Kew Lane, then at a right bend, bear off left by 'The Thatched Cottage' (that isn't!) along a footpath.

5 Join a metalled lane beside the drive to the Coach House then, as the lane curves left, keep ahead beside a house called Woodlands. Follow the path downhill to a stream. Proceed uphill through woodland (Mallards Moor). At a junction of paths on the woodland fringe, bear left with the bridleway, then at a concrete road turn right, then left to join a fenced path between fields.

6 Cross a railway bridge and soon pass a barrier to a road. Keep to the left and after a sharp left-hand bend, look out for a waymarked footpath on your right and follow this path behind some houses for 0.5 mile (800m).

7 Join a metalled path and proceed around modern housing to the end of a cul-de-sac. Follow this out to Hamble Lane, opposite St Andrew's Church and turn left to join the High Street. At the roundabout, bear right down Lower High Street back to the Quay and car park.

Route facts

DISTANCE/TIME
6 miles (9.7km) 3h00

MAP OS Outdoor Leisure 22 New Forest

START Pay-and-display car park by the Quay, Hamble, grid ref: SU 485067

TRACKS Riverside, field and woodland paths, some stretches of road.

GETTING TO THE START
The large village of Hamble is east of Southampton at the end of the B3397, 4 miles (6.4km) south of the M27, junction 8. At a mini-roundabout in the centre of Hamble take the narrow lane downhill to the Quay and car park.

THE PUB The Jolly Sailor, Lands End Road, Old Bursledon. Tel: 023 8040 5557

ⓘ Great care required along the estuary, especially at high tide, and along the roads at Hamble and Bursledon.

NETLEY MAP REF SU4608

Netley, a Victorian town on the shores of the Solent, was formerly important for three things – its castle, its abbey and its gigantic military hospital, the Royal Victoria, built in the aftermath of the Crimean War. This was demolished in 1966, bar the domed royal chapel, and the site is now occupied by the Royal Victoria Country Park which covers more than 100 acres (40ha) of mixed woods, marshes and beach. There is a nature trail, miniature railway and walks.

The ruins of Netley Abbey stand brooding in woodland next to the Solent shore. It was founded here in 1239 as a daughter house of Beaulieu and, as little is known of day to day life here, we must assume a most peaceful and prayerful existence on the part of the monks, until the dissolution of the monasteries. Netley Castle, on the shore near the abbey and formerly the gatehouse, was one of Henry VIII's coastal gun stations – its tall tower is Victorian, and it has been transformed into a wonderful folly with all the panoply of Gothic device (now luxury apartment).

PORTCHESTER CASTLE

MAP REF SU6305

This is one of the most fascinating historical sites in Britain. The massive, 20-foot (6m) high walls of a 3rd-century Roman fort sit on a little promontory on the northern shore of Portsmouth harbour, facing directly across it and out to sea. The thick walls, 10-feet (3m) deep, enclose a large area of 9 acres (3.5ha), and make it the most complete Roman fort in northern Europe.

After the Roman withdrawal from Britain, Portchester's defences were left much as they were until 1133, when a priory was founded here by Henry I. It soon shifted inland to Southwick, but Portchester's parish church is a survivor of the monastic foundation. In 1153 the Normans took over the abandoned fort and built a keep on the northwest corner, plus a wall and moat enclosing an inner bailey. The castle was further fortified at regular intervals throughout history, and in 1415 Henry V mustered his troops on the greensward of the outer bailey and led them all through the Water Gate to embark for France and the Battle of Agincourt. Later it was used as a royal country palace, and in 1535 Henry VIII and Anne Boleyn stayed here and were 'very merry'. During the Napoleonic Wars, around 4,000 French prisoners were held within the walls.

PORTSMOUTH MAP REF SZ6498

Portsmouth has been Britain's foremost naval base since the late 15th century, when it had the first ever dry dock. For a great view over the city, take the lift to the top of the elegant 600-foot (170m) high Spinnaker Tower, opened in 2005.

The town's biggest attraction is the collection of historic ships that can be visited in the Naval Dockyard. HMS *Victory*, launched in 1765, was Nelson's flagship at the Battle of Trafalgar in 1805 and is probably the most famous British warship; she is the oldest commissioned warship in the world. The *Mary Rose*, pride of Henry VIII's fleet, was launched at Portsmouth in 1511, rebuilt to carry more guns in 1536 and sank off Southsea in July 1545, sailing to meet the French in battle, and in full view of the King who was watching from Southsea Castle. The remains of her wreck were finally raised in 1982 and are currently housed in a specially designed and constructed building. 'Permanent conservation' is under way, and there is an exhibition of the artefacts found during salvage. HMS *Warrior*, the first 'ironclad', was launched at Blackwall in 1860, the largest, fastest and most formidable warship the world had ever seen. The Dockyard also houses the redeveloped Royal Naval Museum and 'Action Stations', a thrilling high-tech Royal Naval experience using film and interactive technology.

During World War II Portsmouth was bombed heavily, and it is unfortunate that much of the rebuilding has been particularly uninspired – one building (since demolished) was voted the ugliest in Britain by readers of a certain Sunday newspaper. This being so, hurry through to the historic dockyard and follow the Millennium Promenade (Renaissance Trail) on foot through the bustling Gunwharf Quays shopping complex to The Point. Here is the oldest and most picturesque quarter of Old Portsmouth, where surviving attractive old streets have been restored, and face out onto a little harbour. This area of intricate little roads and Georgian and Victorian houses was known as 'Spice Island', an invocation of the exotic cargoes that arrived here. Walk on the old defences or linger by the seawall in Bath Square to watch the world and the shipping go by – this is the best of Portsmouth.

The city has more than a dozen museums, including Charles Dickens' Birthplace in Old Commercial Road, but the City Museum and Art Gallery found in Museum Road is probably the best place to start. It features 'The Story of Portsmouth' and will point you in the direction of the other remaining historic buildings around the city, including the Landport Gate of 1760, the Square Tower of 1494 and the Royal Garrison Church, where Catherine of Braganza married Charles II in 1662.

There are several good reasons to visit Gosport, just across Portsmouth Harbour, including the view back to Old Portsmouth, and to see the magnificent interior of Holy Trinity Church, which contains the organ once played by Handel. The main attraction, though, is the Royal Navy Submarine Museum, with exhibits relating to underwater warfare and submarine development, and tours of HMS *Alliance*, a submarine completed at the end of World War II. Gosport's Millennium Promenade takes in Timespace, one of the world's largest vertical sundials, erected in 2005, and Explosion!, an exciting, hands-on museum of naval firepower.

■ Activity

HARBOUR TRIPS

Take a relaxing boat trip around the harbour – with an informative running commentary, they give a genuine flavour of seafaring Portsmouth: modern naval vessels, ferries and the general hustle and bustle of this most important of naval ports. IF taking to the sea is not for you, catch the little ferry over to Gosport, for a view back to Old Portsmouth.

SOUTHAMPTON MAP REF SU4213

Modern Southampton has been made by its docks. Its famous double tides give prolonged high water, and although the main container docks are not accessible to the public, there's a grand view of the comings and goings of cruise ships and the pleasure craft from Town Quay and Western Esplanade. This is a sprawling, thriving, working city, with attractions that include some of the best shopping along the south coast, the fine City Art Gallery, a string of leafy green parks, and a little Maritime Museum set in a 15th-century warehouse near the shore, which tells of the great liners built here, and the last, fateful voyage of the RMS *Titanic*. The Solent Sky Aviation Museum, which offers hands-on experience of many of the exhibits (try your hand at a supersonic jet!), was founded in honour of R J Mitchell, designer of the Spitfire fighter plane which was constructed at Southampton's Supermarine Works A flying boat in the collection is another reminder of the port's history.

Southampton was very badly hit by bombing during World War II, and much rebuilding was done in haste and very cheaply. As a result, it is an unattractive architectural mishmash, but there are some historic gems from all periods.

The most interesting area lies south of the gleaming West Quay shopping centre, and it is worth parking there to explore on foot. The mall has many well-known street shops, including John Lewis, Waitrose and Marks & Spencer, and leads out onto Above Bar Street, a pedestrianised shopping street set above a bulky gateway, one of several

last surviving fragments of the medieval walled city. Stroll down here, passing the Dolphin Hotel – novelist Jane Austen celebrated her 18th birthday on the first-floor ballroom here in 1793. Next door is the bombed-out Church of the Holy Rood, now dedicated to the merchant seamen of the city, and including a memorial to the 500 local crew who died aboard HMS *Titanic* when she sank in 1912. Beyond nearby St Michael's, the oldest church in the city, dating to 1070, and the only one undamaged in the war, lie Bugle Street and French Street, with the Medieval Merchant's House of 1290 and the striking timbered Tudor House Museum and Garden. Another little interesting corner to explore is Oxford Street, behind Queen's Terrace, its mellow old houses now filled with trendy restaurants, and with an Edwardian pub, the London Hotel, at one corner.

On the shore, ferries leave for the Isle of Wight and Hythe, and Ocean Village is a modern marina from where you can take a cruise of the harbour.

SOUTHSEA MAP REF SZ6698

Beyond the tangle of Old Portsmouth's streets to the east, you emerge on to Southsea Common, faced by imposing terraces of 19th-century stucco. The grassy common overlooking the sea escaped development during the 19th century because it was used for military training, and for this we must be very grateful as it gives Southsea its own distinctive flavour. Southsea developed as a residential suburb of Portsmouth, but the seaside location transformed it into a holiday place from the 1860s.

Today there is a raucous funfair at Clarence Pier. The wide Clarence Esplanade, between the common and the sea, has the fabulous Blue Reef Aquarium, the big Naval War Memorial and the Southsea Castle Museum. Near by, the D-Day Museum contains the remarkable Overlord Embroidery, a fine tapestry depicting the Allied invasion of Normandy in June 1944, paying homage to the Bayeux Tapestry of 1066.

Further east the pier provides boat trips and amusements, while on East Parade is the Cumberland House Natural History Museum. The Royal Marines Museum is housed in Eastney Barracks, beyond which are the Port Solent and Eastney Marinas. The Solent Way passes along the Southsea front.

During the 1860s four sea forts were built offshore, part of the ring of forts to protect Portsmouth and Spithead from a feared attack by the French. The smallest is Spitbank Fort, which had provision for nine 38-ton guns and can be visited by ferry from Southsea pier.

TITCHFIELD MAP REF SU5405

Titchfield, on the lower reaches of the River Meon, is a lovely village of twisting roads with a charming High Street. The aerospace factories on its outskirts create a curious juxtaposition of ancient and modern. In medieval times Titchfield was a market centre and a prosperous port, with a large and thriving abbey, founded in 1232. At the Dissolution the abbey passed to Thomas Wriothesley, the 1st Earl of Southampton, who then converted part of it into a house, but it fell into disrepair in the 18th century and

■ Activity

THE SOLENT WAY
This 60-mile (96km) path runs from Milford on Sea via Southampton and Portsmouth to the wild saltings of Langstone Harbour and Emsworth. The stretch from Warsash (or Hamble) to Emsworth begins along an undeveloped stretch of Solent coast between the Hamble River and Titchfield Haven, at the mouth of the River Meon, where there is a nature reserve. Beyond Titchfield Haven it goes past the beach at Lee-on-the-Solent and the lovely curve of Stokes Bay, turning inland at Gilkicker Point for the ferry from Gosport to Old Portsmouth. From here it passes Southsea to the edge of Langstone Harbour, before curving to Emsworth.

is now in ruins, split off from the village by the A27. Little of the original abbey remains but a huge Tudor gatehouse. A 15th-century tithe barn stands near by.

The 1st Earl also instituted a land reclamation scheme, damming the mouth of the river and building a canal. One of England's earliest canals, it was too small for merchant ships and Titchfield's days as a port were soon over. The Earl has not been forgiven, and his effigy is burnt at celebrations in October organised by the Bonfire Boys.

A different – and magnificent – effigy of the Earl can be found in the south chapel of the church. The detailed Wriothesley Monument by artist Gerard Johnson, a Flemish refugee, was carved in 1594 and shows the 1st Earl with his wife and son. The 3rd Earl was a friend of William Shakespeare, and it is said that some of his plays received their first performance here.

Ports Down and Southwick

Ports Down rises 381ft (116m) above the coastal plain and extends for some 6.25 miles (10.1km) from Bedhampton to Fareham. It commands impressive views over Portsmouth and Langstone Harbours. This route climbs the backslope of the hill to Nelson's Monument. Hundreds of boats were assembled along Hampshire's low coastline and harbours ready for the D-Day invasion in June 1944. The planning of Operation Overlord was undertaken in secrecy from the sleepy village of Southwick.

Route Directions

1 From the village car park turn right to a junction and bear left to a roundabout. Go straight over and then take Crooked Walk Lane towards Portchester. Climb steeply, bearing right by a quarry.

2 Where the road veers sharp left, briefly take Portchester Lane right. Almost straight away turn left through a gap in the verge and follow the footpath across a field, heading for the corner of a copse. Skirt the copse and cross a stile. Heading towards Nelson's Monument across a field to a stile and lane. Turn left, pass Nelson's Monument and turn right at the cross-roads, signed to Fort Nelson.

3 Having visited the fort, retrace your steps back to the Monument and continue down the lane for 50yds (46m). Take the footpath left over a stile. Follow the path indicated by the official diversion sign to the right corner of the fort, cross a stile and skirt the edge of the fort to a further stile. Bear half-right across the field, between a house and pylon, to a road.

4 Turn right downhill, then right again at the next junction. After some 200yds

(183m) bear left through St Nicholas's churchyard. Rejoin the road and continue past barns and a pond. Shortly, beside a lay-by, bear left over a stile and follow the footpath along the left-hand field edge. Continue on between fields, then by Grub Coppice to cross a bridge.

5 Climb a stile, and keep to the right-hand field edge to a stile on the right. Cross a further stile and walk along the left-hand field edge. Turn left across a stile by the stream and bear right, around the edge of the field to a stile and road. Cross the stile opposite and then walk along the right-hand field edge close to a stream. Follow the field boundary as it swings left, pass a gate to the next field, and shortly bear right across a stile and bridge to join a track.

6 Pass between farm buildings, then go through a gate and eventually bear left down to the B2177. Cross over the road and take the footpath right along a track. It soon becomes grassy and bears right into woodland. Take the second footpath on the left, emerge from the trees and then head across a narrow field. Cross a bridge, bear

right, then bear half-left making for a large oak tree. Descend steps to a lane.

7 Cross over and bear half-right across the field towards the church tower. Cross a bridge and continue through a plantation. Beyond another bridge, walk up a drive to the road. Turn left, then right into Southwick to pass The Red Lion. Keep left at the junction and left again to the car park.

Route facts

DISTANCE/TIME
6 miles (9.7km) 3h

MAP OS Explorer 119 Meon Valley

START Free car park by the village hall, Southwick, close to HMS Dryad, grid ref: SU 627085

TRACKS Field, woodland paths and stretches of road, 15 stiles

GETTING TO THE START
Southwick is a village north of Portsmouth. It lies just north off the B2177 between Wickham and Purbrook. In the village follow signs for HMS *Dryad*, to find the village hall car park.

THE PUB The Red Lion, High Street, Southwick. Tel: 023 9237 7223

❶ Two fairly busy sections of lane with no pavement. Suitable for older, more experienced family groups.

■ TOURIST INFORMATION CENTRES

Fareham
Westbury Manor,
84 West Street.
Tel: 01329 221343

Portsmouth
Clarence Esplanade,
Southsea.
Tel: 023 9282 6722

Southampton
9 Civic Centre Road.
Tel: 023 8083 3333;
www.visit-southampton.co.uk

■ PLACES OF INTEREST

Burseldon Brickworks
Swanwick Lane, Swanwick.
Tel: 01489 576248

Bursledon Windmill
Windmill Lane, Bursledon.
Tel: 023 8040 4999;
www.hants.gov.uk/museum/
windmill

Charles Dickens' Birthplace
393 Old Commercial Road,
Portsmouth.
Tel: 023 9282 7261;
www.charlesdickensbirthplac
e.co.uk

City Museum and Art Gallery
Museum Road, Portsmouth.
Tel: 023 9282 7261;
www.portsmouthcity
museums.co.uk

Cumberland House Natural History Museum
Eastern Parade, Southsea.
Tel: 023 9282 7261;
www.chnhm.co.uk
Free.

D-Day Museum & Ovelord Embroidery
Clarence Esplanade,
Southsea.
Tel: 023 9282 7261;
www.ddaymuseum.co.uk

Explosion! Museum of Naval Firepower
Priddy's Hard, Gosport.
Tel: 023 9250 5600;
www.explosion.org.uk

Hawthorns Urban Wildlife Centre
Southampton Common.
Tel: 023 8067 1921; www.
southampton.gov.uk/leisure
Free.

Manor Farm Country Park & Farm Museum
Pylands Lane, Bursledon.
Tel: 01489 787055;
www.hants.gov.uk/manorfarm

Maritime Museum
Town Quay, Southampton.
Tel: 023 8063 5904
Free.

Netley Abbey (EH)
Tel: 023 8045 5157. Free.

Portchester Castle (EH)
Castle Street, Portchester.
Tel: 0239 237 8291

Portsmouth Historic Dockyard
Victory Gate, HM Naval Base.
Tel: 023 9286 1512/9766;
www.historicdockyard.co.uk

Royal Armouries
Fort Nelson, Portsdown Hill
Road, Fareham.
Tel: 01392 233734;
www.royalarmouries.org

Royal Marines Museum
Southsea.
Tel: 023 9281 9385; www.
royalmarinesmuseum.co.uk

Royal Navy Submarine Museum
Haslar Jetty Road, Gosport.
Tel: 023 9252 9217;
www.rnsubmus.co.uk

Royal Victoria Country Park
Tel: 023 8045 5157;
www.hants.gov.uk/rvcp

Southampton City Art Gallery
Civic Centre.
Tel: 023 8083 2277;
www.southampton.gov.uk/art

Southsea Castle Museum
Clarence Esplanade.
Tel: 023 9282 7261;
www.southseacastle.co.uk

Spinnaker Tower
Gunwharf Quays,
Portsmouth.
Tel: 02392 857520;
www.spinnakertower.co.uk

Titchfield Haven National Nature Reserve
Hill Head, by Stubbington.
Tel: 01329 662145;
www.hants.gov.uk/titchfield

Wickham Vineyard
Botley Road, Shedfield.
Tel: 01329 834042;
www.wickhamvineyard.co.uk

■ FOR CHILDREN

Blue Reef Aquarium
Clarence Esplanade,
Southsea.
Tel: 023 9287 5222;
www.bluereefaquarium.co.uk

Hampshire Mega-Maze
Forty Acres Farm, Havant
Road, Havant.
Tel: 023 9247 2854;
www.forty-acres.co.uk

The Pyramids Centre
Clarence Esplanade,
Southsea.
Tel: 023 9279 9977;
www.pyramids.co.uk

■ SHOPPING

Bargate Markets
Bargate, Southampton.
Friday market, plus Farmers
Markets one Sat per month
(www.hampshirefarmersmar
kets.co.uk). There are artists
Markets on the last Sun of
each month
(www.eatsouthampton.com).

Gunwharf Quays
www.gunwharf-quays.com

**The Mall Marlands Shopping
Centre**
Civic Centre Road,
Southampton.
Tel: 023 8033 9164;
www.themall.co.uk/marlands

West Quay Shopping Centre
Tel: 023 8033 6828;
www.west-quay.co.uk

**Whitely Village Outlet
Shopping**
Close to junction 9, M27.

■ PERFORMING ARTS

Kings Theatre
Albert Road, Southsea.
Tel: 023 92 828282
www.kings-southsea.com

The Mayflower
Commercial Road,
Southampton.
Tel: 023 8071 1811
www.the-mayflower.com

New Theatre Royal
20–24 Guildhall Walk,
Portsmouth.
Tel: 023 9264 9000
www.newtheatreroyal.com

Nuffield Theatre
University Road,
Southampton.
Tel: 023 8067 1771

■ SPORTS & ACTIVITIES

BOAT TRIPS

Blue Funnel Cruises
Ocean Village, Southampton.
Tel: 023 8022 3278;
www.bluefunnel.co.uk

Blue Star Boats
River Hamble
Tel: 023 8045 3542;
www.bluestarboats.co.uk

SS *Shieldhall*
47 Berth, Eastern Dock,
Southampton, Dock Gate 4.
Tel: 023 8022 5853;
www.ss-shieldhall.co.uk

HORSE-RIDING

**Gleneagles Equestrian
Centre**
Allington Lane, West End,
Southampton.
Tel: 023 8047 3370

WALKING

The Solent Way
A 60-mile (96km) long-
distance walk from Milford on
Sea to Emsworth.

Hayling Billy Trail
A 4-mile (6km) trail between
Havant and Langston.

The Strawberry Trail
15-mile (24km) circular walk
in the Hamble Valley.

■ ANNUAL CUSTOMS
& EVENTS

Botley
Summer Festival, end Jun.

Hamble Week
Carnival week, early Jul.
Tel: 023 8045 7935;
www.hambleevents.org.uk

Netley
Fireworks Spectacular, Royal
Victoria Country Park, around
5 Nov.
Tel: 023 8045 5157

**Netley Marsh Steam & Craft
Show**
Mid-Jul. Meadow Mead
Farm. Tel: 023 8086 7882;
www.netleymarshsteamandcr
aftshow.org.

Southampton
Annual Kite Festival, mid-Jun
at Lordshill.

**The Big Southampton Boat
Show**
Mid-Sep. Tel: 0870 060 0246

**Swanwick, Bursledon and
Warsash Regatta**
Around Elephant Boatyard,
end Aug.
Tel: 023 8045 6969;
www.bursledonregatta.co.uk.

Titchfield
Carnival and bonfire, last
Mon in Oct.

Tea Rooms

Country Kitchens Tea Rooms

6 High Street, Botley,
SO30 2EA
Tel: 01489 789161

Drop into this village tea room for cream teas in summer, plus hot and cold food and sandwiches.

The Pantry Tea Room

Manor Farm Country Park,
Pylands Lane, Bursledon,
SO30 2ER
Tel: 01489 787055

In a perfect rural setting of this old farmstead, tuck into a snack, ice cream or a full-blown, home-cooked meal.

Tower Café Bar

Spinnaker Tower, Gunwharf Quays, Portsmouth, PO1 3TT
Tel: 02392 857520;
www.spinnakertower.co.uk

Take your morning coffee or afternoon tea in style (not at the top!) in Portsmouth's newest venue. Sandwiches and cakes give way to wine and beer in the evenings, as you sit and watch the sun go down over the harbour.

The Village Tea Rooms

High Street, Hamble,
SO31 4HA
Tel: 023 8045 5583

Just down from the main square in the village, in a 300-year old house that was once the local coffin-maker's premises, this cosy tea room doubles as a gift shop and gallery of local art and crafts, and spills out into the pretty back garden in summer. Try the Hamble Cream Special, with scones, cream and preserves, or home-made cakes and shortbread, or come early for the Skipper's Choice Breakfast.

Pubs

The Cowherds

The Common, Southampton,
SO15 7NN
Tel: 023 8051 6921

On the A33, at the heart of Southampton Common, this pub was once the haunt of cattle drovers on their way to London. Now it's the perfect spot for lunch or dinner – try the ham hock with mustard sauce, or perhaps the pork, apple and cider sausages with Cheddar mash. There's a patio outside and inside it's cosy with open fires, oak beams and wood panelling.

Greens Restaurant & Pub

The Square, Wickham,
PO17 5JQ
Tel: 01329 833197

Set on a coner of Wickham's picturesque square, and close to the River Meon, the menus at this mock-Tudor pub make good use of fresh ingredients, from smoked duck salad with pear chutney to delicious apricot-glazed bread-and-butter pudding. Food is not served on Mondays. Beers include Hopback Summer Lightning and Fullers London Pride.

The Jolly Sailor

Lands End Road, Burseldon,
SO31 8DN
Tel: 023 8040 5557

This appealing old pub, overlooking Hamble marina, achieved fame in the 1980s as a location for BBC TV's salty soap opera, *Howard's Way*. The menus include a variety of offerings, from *moules marinière* and *bouillabaisse* to chunky sandwiches. Beers include Fursty Ferret and Tanglefoot.

The Still & West

2 Bath Square, Old Portsmouth, PO1 2JL
Tel: 023 9282 1567

At the top of Broad Street, and close to HMS *Victory*, this nautically themed 1504 pub has great views over the harbour and to the Isle of Wight. As you might expect, there's lots of fish on the menu, including a trademark grill of fresh fish and mussels, and seafood paella.

Winchester & Salisbury

ALRESFORD ■ AMPFIELD ■ AVINGTON PARK ■ WALK 9

FARLEY MOUNT ■ MOTTISFONT ■ ROMSEY ■ SALISBURY

CAR TOUR 2 ■ WALK 10 ■ SHAFTESBURY ■ STOCKBRIDGE

WINCHESTER

Winchester, England's ancient capital, lies amid rolling chalkland scenery, with roads radiating outwards from it across the county. Surrounding it, particularly to the north and west, are two contrasting landscapes: the wide serene chalklands of 'High Hampshire', lonely and open, dotted here and there with clumps of dark green yews and graceful beeches, and the fisherman's Hampshire – shallow green valleys of water meadows and sparkling streams that bring anglers from the four winds to try their skill in England's most famous trout rivers. This is an area of unhurried little roads, great houses and gardens, tranquil rivers and sweeping views.

9 Walk start point

2 Tour start point

RIVER TEST

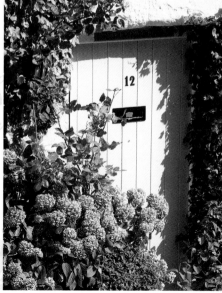

Unmissable attractions

Stroll in lovely Hilier Gardens, where you will witness a blaze of colour whatever the season...gain an insight into the life of Lord Mountbatten at Broadlands magnificent mansion...savour the haunting atmosphere of Salisbury Cathedral as you listen to the pure harmonies of its choir...test your stamina by climbing Shaftesbury's much-photographed and filmed, cobbled Gold Hill...admire the grandeur of Mottisfont Abbey amble beside the sparkling watercress beds at Alresford...fly-fish for trout on the RIver Test then retreat to The Mayfly to swap stories of 'the one that got away'...visit the cathedral city of Winchester, steeped in historical fact and folklore.

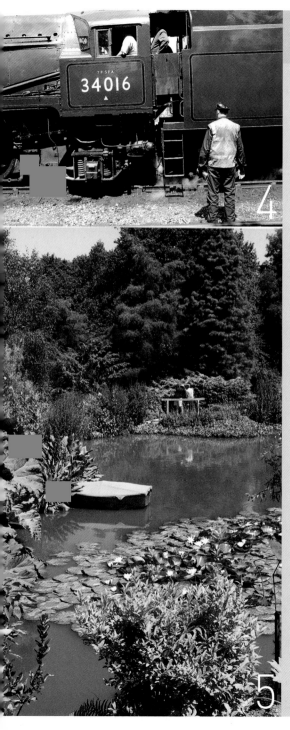

1 Salisbury Cathedral
Building work on the cathedral began in 1220; an army of labourers and craftsmen toiled for around 40 years. The tower and famous spire were added in the 14th century.

2 Great Hall, Winchester
The only remaining intact part of Winchester Castle now houses the top of a painted table. Once claimed as King Arthur's famous Round Table, tests have shown that it probably dates from Tudor times.

3 Old Sarum
William the Conqueror erected a castle here soon after his arrival in England. Eventually a cathedral was built in the grounds but in the 13th century this was moved to nearby Salisbury; the castle eventually went into decline.

4 Watercress Line
The great days of steam rail travel has been revived on this line which runs between Arlesford and Alton. When constructed in the mid-19th century, the line ran from Winchester to Alton. The track and trains are maintained by enthusiastic volunteers.

5 Hillier Gardens
Sir Harold Hillier established his arboretum in 1953 in the grounds of his home. The stunning plant collection extends over 180 acres (72ha).

ALRESFORD MAP REF SU3832

Lovely Alresford, with its wide streets of friendly Georgian houses of brick and stucco, lies in the broad valley of the River Alre, hence the name (pronounced 'Allsford'). It is really two places – Old Alresford to the north of the river, which is now no more than a village with an adjoining park, and New Alresford, the busy market town to the south which was 'New' in about 1200. Between the two is Alresford Pond, created by Bishop de Lucy in the 13th century. Its dam, the Great Weir, is the largest non-military medieval earthwork in England and the only one that still serves this original dual purpose of dam and road causeway. Today its 30 acres (12ha) are a haven for wildlife and also feed the famous local watercress beds.

New Alresford retains its medieval street plan, with a T-shape formed by the spacious elegant Broad Street and West and East Streets, the old Winchester–London road. A borough by 1294, New Alresford soon became one of England's ten greatest wool markets. Two of its mills survive, the Town Mill and the old Fulling Mill. Fires devastated New Alresford between the early 15th century and 1689, which accounts for its mainly Georgian appearance.

Approach from Old Alresford or from Bishop's Sutton for the most attractive introduction to the town – the south approach from Cheriton leads through less inviting modern suburbs. Strolling through New Alresford is a delight. The town has a variety of interesting shops and some excellent craft workshops, and Broad Street, with its line of lime trees and pretty old fashioned lamps, is one of Hampshire's finest streets.

Mary Russell Mitford, author of the classic *Our Village*, was born at 27 Broad Street in 1787 and lived there until she was ten, when she moved with her father to Three Mile Cross near Reading – the village of her book. She later wrote, 'Alresford is or will be celebrated in history for two things: the first, to speak modestly, is my birth, the second is cricket'. Few today would associate Alresford with cricket, but Taylor of Alresford, a member of the famous Hambledon Club was born here, and cricket writer and commentator John Arlott once lived at the Old Sun. Today Alresford is better known for its watercress beds and its steam railway, the Watercress Line.

North of Alresford, Northington Grange is the dramatic empty shell of a neoclassical mansion, where the 1999 movie *Onegin* was filmed.

■ **Insight**

HAMPSHIRE WATERCRESS

Watercress needs to be planted submerged in gently flowing shallow water if it is to be grown to perfection, and few places have exactly the right conditions. The Hampshire chalklands with their sparkling streams fit the bill precisely, particularly around Alresford where the plants flourish in specially constructed beds alongside the streams. Watercress needs to be consumed soon after it is picked because it wilts easily; the Watercress Line, now a preserved steam railway, originally carried the harvest to London markets; today container lorries transport it to the European market.

AMPFIELD MAP REF SU4023

In rolling countryside to the southwest of Winchester, this little village, set among beech woods and vast cornfields, is best known for the nearby Hillier Gardens. Sir Harold Hillier, the great plantsman, began his famous collection of trees and shrubs on the Ampfield estate in 1953. It became one of the largest in the world, with some 40,000 temperate plants originating from every continent. There is colour at every season of the year with witch hazels, rhododendrons, autumn foliage and herbaceous perennials.

The heart of the village is at Knapp, now designated a conservation area. There were clay pits and a pottery near by, and the well-known Potters Heron Hotel preserves in its name a shadowy recollection of the old industry, since a potter's treadle wheel is also known as a 'hern' or 'heron'. In much later times this same clay was used to make the bricks for the Church of St Mark, built between 1838 and 1841 at the instigation of John Keble, a famous member of the High Church Oxford Movement, who was vicar at nearby Hursley.

Ampfield has literary associations. Richard Morley, the 17th-century 'Hedge Poet', lived here and the Rev W Awdry, author of the 'Thomas the Tank Engine' books, spent his boyhood in Ampfield, where his father was the vicar.

AVINGTON PARK

MAP REF SU5432

Avington Park lies between Easton and Alresford, east of Winchester. Dating mainly to the early 18th century, but with some parts much earlier, it is a

big rose-pink house with a splendid portico and some wonderful interior features, including a painted ceiling by Verrio and a fine colonnade in the 19th-century conservatory. In November 1825 William Cobbett rode through on his way from Easton, and described the scene: '...The house is close down at the edge of the meadow land; there is a lawn before it, and a pond supplied by the Itchen...We looked down on all this from a rising ground, and the water, like a looking-glass, showed us the trees, and even the animals. This certainly is one of the prettiest spots in the world...'The views to the house across the lake and parkland seem little changed.

The brick-built Church of St Mary was built in from 1768 to 1771 by Margaret, Marchioness of Carnarvon. It preserves the air of the 18th century as verily as the view over the park. A large monument to the Marchioness, who died in 1768, is in pink and white marble with two urns and an obelisk. Another monument is to John Shelley, brother of the famous poet, who purchased Avington Park in 1847.

A walk around the Alresfords

New Alresford is one of Hampshire's most picturesque small towns. Much of the architecture is Georgian, and a stroll around the three principal streets reveals a traditional country town shops plus specialist clothes, antiquarian books and craft shops. Close to both Old and New Alresford you will find a network of crystal clear chalk streams, rivulets and channels that form the rivers Arle and Itchen and the Candover Stream. Since Victorian times these springs and rivers have played a vital role in the production of making Alresford the 'Watercress Capital' of England, and the steam railway once transported watercress across the country.

Route Directions

1 From the car park walk down Station Road to the T-junction with West Street. Turn right, then left down Broad Street and keep left at the bottom along Mill Hill. Half-way down follow the Wayfarer's Walk marker left down Ladywell Lane and soon join the riverbank and pass the timbered and thatched Fulling Mill Cottage which straddles the River Arle. At the bottom of Broad Street is The Globe on the Lake pub where you can stop for a drink or a meal before you continue on your walk.

2 Continue to the bottom of Dean Lane and turn right, keeping to the riverside path. Cross a footbridge over the river, and ascend to pass by some cottages. Soon after, follow the footpath that skirts a private drive, bear off to the left and follow it along the field edge. Join a minor road and shortly bear right up a stony track, signed Wayfarer's Walk. At a junction of tracks turn right (the Wayfarer's Walk goes left) and ascend to a minor road.

3 Turn left, walk down until you get to Fobdown Farm and then take the lane on the right beside the farm buildings,

signposted 'Right of Way'. Continue along the stony track, then on reaching a T-junction of tracks, turn to the right and follow the worn track for just over 0.5 mile (80om), gently descending into Old Alresford.

4 Pass watercress beds on your right, and follow the now metalled lane left, past some houses. Turn right beside the green to the B3046. Cross straight over and up to the metalled path, turning right to reach a lane opposite St Mary's Church.

5 After visiting the fine 18th-century church, cross over the road and turn left along a pavement to get to the grass triangle by a junction. Bear right along the lane and take the footpath ahead over a stream and beside watercress beds back to Mill Lane and Broad Street.

Route facts

DISTANCE/TIME
4 miles (6.4km) 1h45

MAP OS Explorer 132 Winchester

START Pay car park off Station Road, New Alresford, grid ref: SU 588325

TRACKS Riverside paths, tracks, field, woodland paths and roads

GETTING TO THE START New Alresford is signposted off the A31 between Winchester and Alton, 6 miles (9.7km) east of Winchester. On the main village street, follow signs to the Watercress Line to locate the parking area.

THE PUB The Globe on the Lake, The Soke, Broad Street, Alresford.
Tel: 01962 732294;
www.globeonthelake.co.uk

❶ Alresford can be busy with cars; some riverside paths; take care crossing the B3046. Suitable for all ages.

■ Insight

THE SILVER ROUTE

The Roman road from the Mendip mines via Old Sarum and Winchester crosses Farley Mount. This road was once used to transport the precious silver-bearing lead to Bitterne, now a suburb of Southampton, for shipment to the Roman Imperial Mint at Lyon. Today, this important road can be traced eastwards as an embankment under the trees, but once you get nearer to Winchester it is followed by the present-day Sarum Road.

FARLEY MOUNT MAP REF SU4029

Farley Mount Country Park covers over 1,000 acres (405ha) of chalk upland west of Winchester and east of the broad Test valley. At 586 feet (178m), it remains the highest point in the region and there are wonderful views in all directions. Its most prominent feature is the pyramid folly, a memorial raised in 1734 to a horse who bravely won its race despite having fallen the previous day into a chalk pit while out hunting. The horse was renamed Beware Chalk Pit.

This popular country park is best known for its variety of habitats, with short turf, mixed woodland and Forestry Commission plantation. There is plenty of wildlife in the old oak, beech and yew woods and also in the great swathes of ancient coppicing. Orchids are plentiful and there are a number of nature trails in Crab Wood, on the east side of the park. Car parks are clearly marked. The park is crossed by the Roman road from the Mendip silver-lead mines and Old Sarum to Winchester, and by the Clarendon Way long-distance footpath.

MOTTISFONT MAP REF SU3226

The little village of Mottisfont lies in that part of the wide green Test valley where the trees seem to be exceptionally large, the streams of the river are particularly numerous and the atmosphere breathes peace and prosperity. The village's name is derived from the spring or 'font' which rises where the village 'moot' was held in Saxon times.

A house of Augustinian canons was founded here in 1201, which at the Dissolution passed to Lord Sandys, in exchange for the then villages of Paddington and Chelsea. Unusually, it was the church that he converted into his mansion, demolishing the residential parts of the priory. The Tudor building was remodelled in the 18th century by the Mills family, to whom it had passed, giving rise to the present mellow house.

Today Mottisfont Abbey is famed for its drawing room, decorated in Gothic trompe l'oeil style by Rex Whistler in 1938, and for Derek Hill's 20th-century picture collection. The tranquil grounds have sweeping lawns which run down to the River Test, and the walled garden houses the superb National Collection of old roses, at their best in June.

ROMSEY MAP REF SU3521

This small town on the River Test is dominated by its magnificent Abbey Church of 1120–70, a handsome Norman building with a low, square tower, massive walls, a splendid south doorway and an interior of beautifully carved Norman arches. It contains two remarkable Saxon stone carvings from earlier churches on the site, and its treasures include the Romsey Psalter (a 15th-century illuminated manuscript), and a monument to the noted economist Sir William Petty (1623–87), born in Romsey and a founder member of the Royal Society. Lord Mountbatten of Burma (1900–79), one-time confidant to Prince Charles, is buried in the abbey.

Romsey is an attractive place with many unobtrusively pleasing streets of Georgian and later houses. It centres on spacious Market Place, which has a statue in the middle of Lord Palmerston, the Victorian statesman who lived at Broadlands. The 13th-century timbered King John's House, opposite the Abbey Church, is said to be where John's daughter lived before she married the Scottish king. There is a lovely park with a bandstand, beside the River Test.

Across the river are the gates of Broadlands, a Palladian mansion with a great 18th-century portico, set in a landscaped park that was created by 'Capability' Brown. Once the home of Lord Palmerston, more recently of Lord Mountbatten and now of Lord Romsey, it houses exhibitions on Mountbatten's life and a spectacular Mountbatten audio-visual presentation in the stable block. The house contains many fine works of art including several pieces by Van Dycks. Rooms include the stately Saloon and a powder-blue Wedgwood Room. Furniture by Ince and Mayhew was made specifically for the house.

To the east, the churchyard of East Wellow contains the grave of Florence Nightingale (1820–1920), the founder of modern nursing. The church has some unusual 13th-century wall paintings.

■ Visit

ROMSEY ABBEY

The nuns of Romsey Abbey were almost wiped out by the Black Death, and after the Dissolution the church was purchased by the people of Romsey who, until then, had worshipped under sufferance in the north transept. We must be grateful to those Tudor townsfolk who raised the necessary £100 to buy the church, since not only Hampshire but all England would be the poorer without this wonderful parish church, the largest in the county.

■ Visit

CATHEDRAL CHOIR

There has been a choir at Salisbury Cathedral for around 800 years, and today it is famous for admitting girls as well as boys. Children as young as seven years old can join the choir school, taking part in regular lessons alongside their daily two singing practices. Hear them during term time at evensong and at special services throughout the year.

SALISBURY MAP REF SU1530

Old Sarum's history dates back to a time long before records were made, and the giant earthwork is founded on an Iron Age camp that covered around 56 acres. The earliest settlers were followed by Romans, Anglo-Saxons, Danes and Norman – William the Conqueror is said to have reviewed his troops here in 1070.

A Norman castle and cathedral were erected, but water was scarce on this plain, and the military and ecclesiastical factions could not agree who should take precedence. Accordingly, in 1220 a new cathedral was planned to the south in nearby New Sarum – or Salisbury –

using stones from the old one. It seems that the spirit went out of Old Sarum in more ways than one, as the castle fell into decay, and the town was gradually abandoned. There's not much to see of this once-thriving settlement today, but for the excavated foundations of the old cathedral and fragments of the castle.

And so, while Winchester's old heart may seem like a medieval muddle, Salisbury feels comparatively spacious and regular – it was planned and built on a grid structure, beside the River Avon. Many old streets are named after the goods that were sold there – Fish Row, Butchers Row, and so on. Some have been pedestrianised, and highlights to look out for include the 16th-century façade of the Joiner's Hall on St Ann Street and the 18th-century Guildhall. The Poultry Cross in Silver Street dates to the 15th century.

Unusually, the Gothic cathedral was built in almost one go, the majority of it being completed by 1258, at a cost of around £27,000. The main exception is its soaring spire, 404ft (123m) high, which was added in the 14th century and is the structure's most identifiable feature, painted most memorably by John Constable from across the water meadows in 1823. A climb up 332 steps and through the cathedral's roof spaces takes you to the top of the tower for far-reaching views over the city and around.

Salisbury cathedral's interior was unfortunately drastically remodelled in the 18th century by James Wyatt, who 'decluttered' it by clearing screens and tombs and throwing out some of the old stained glass. Wyatt also covered over the 13th-century roof painting in the choir, but this was later restored. Today the most striking glass is the intense blue 'Prisoners of Conscience Window' in the Trinity Chapel.

Two of the cathedral's most prized possessions are the clock of 1386, the oldest in England, and an original copy of the Magna Carta, the 'great document' forced by rebellious barons on King John at Runnymede in 1215, to limit the monarch's more arbitrary powers. It's surprisingly small for such a significant document, about A3 size.

A stroll around the extensive cathedral close is essential, including gracious old houses such as the Old Deanery, and the King's House, now home to the interesting Salisbury and South Wiltshire Museum, which includes finds from Stonehenge, watercolours by Turner, history relating to Old Sarum, and the Warminster Jewel. Mompesson House is a gem in Queen Anne style, with notable plasterwork and a pretty walled garden, and played a starring role in the 1995 film of Jane Austen's *Sense and Sensibility*. The Wardrobe contains a military museum.

The 17th-century Palladian mansion of Wilton House, home of the Earl of Pembroke, lies west of the town, and is well worth a look for its famous Single and Double Cube Rooms and its elegant gardens. The house was also the most unlikely setting for the D-Day landings headquarters during World War II; more recently, scenes from *Sense and Sensibility*, *The Madness of King George*, *Mrs Brown* and the 2005 movie *Pride and Prejudice* were filmed here.

Along the Romantic Road

This circular route links the historic centres of Winchester and Salisbury, with their fine cathedrals, and the market towns of Stockbridge and Romsey, set deep in the beautiful Test Valley. The drive takes you through rolling countryside and passes many pretty villages. Along the way you will pass some of the area's most attractive houses and gardens, and if you have time, it's worth stopping at one or two places to stretch your legs and appreciate all these magnificent homes have to offer.

Route Directions

1 Leave the centre of Winchester, following signs for Romsey and the A3090. Pass the hospital, go straight on at a roundabout, and bear right at the next, signed to Romsey. Pass a golf course, left, go through Pitt and down a long hill, to turn right just before the village of Standon, signed to Farley Mount and Sparsholt. Very soon turn left, signed Farley Mount, and follow this narrow country lane through trees to the open hilltops for 2 miles (3km) to reach Farley Mount Country Park. Keep left.
There are several car parks on your right where you can stop and visit the country park. The folly monument is up to your left.

2 The road descends steadily through beautiful chalky landscape. Go through the pretty village of Ashley with its white-painted church and old well. Bear left at the end of the village for Kings Somborne and Romsey. At the

next junction bear left, and go through the village of Kings Somborne with its pretty thatched houses. Turn right at the end, and right again in front of the Crown Inn onto the A3057. Follow this for three miles to a junction on the edge of Stockbridge and turn left at the roundabout, signed Salisbury. Go through Stockbridge, cross the River Test and immediately turn left on a minor road, signed Houghton. This road runs largely parallel with the river. The village of Houghton is long and spread out. Look out for Houghton Lodge, on your left, with its glorious gardens and lawns sweeping down to the River Test.

3 Continue past the black-and-white timbered Boot Inn. After 2.5 miles (4km) reach a junction. Turn right for Dunbridge, and keep going straight ahead for Mottisfont. Continue on this narrow road through rolling farmland into Mottisfont village. Go straight

on through to visit the famous Abbey and gardens.
In a picturesque setting by the River Test, Mottisfont Abbey is adapted from a 12th-century priory. In the gardens are the National Collection of old-fashioned roses.

4 Retrace your route through the village and turn left on Bengers Lane, signed to Dunbridge and Broughton. At the junction with the B3084 turn left down Hatt Hill and go downhill into Dunbridge. Cross the river and railway line and turn right, signed to Lockerley. At the junction in Lockerley turn right, signed East Tytherley, pass under the railway and then turn left after the church, for East and West Dean. Pass through Lockerley Green.
The hamlet of Lockerley Green is built around a large village green.

5 Cross the railway, pass through East Dean village, and West Dean with its lumber yard and thatched cottages. Turn left by the old brick bridge, signed East Grimstead and Salisbury. Go straight ahead at the junction for East Grimstead, then go under the railway and soon you enter East Grimstead, with its neat little flint church. Turn left, signed West Grimstead and Salisbury, and keep straight on this road, proceeding through wooded Alderbury. At the junction turn right for Salisbury, and continue downhill to meet the A36. Turn left and follow this into the middle of Salisbury, following signs round the ring road to the Central Car Park. Explore the medieval city on foot taking in the cathedral and the museums that are housed in some of the historic buildings in Cathedral Close.

6 Leave Salisbury on the A36, signed to Southampton. Once you get to the end of the dual carriageway, look out for the viewpoint of Pepperbox Hill to your left. Descend to traffic lights and turn left on the A27, signed to Romsey and Whiteparish. Pass through Whiteparish, with its handsome old houses, and a string of hamlets that follow including Sherfield English. Look out for the bulky Abbey on your left as you descend further towards Romsey. At the junction turn left, signed Romsey and Winchester. Cross the River Test and, when you reach the roundabout by Broadlands, make a left turn to Romsey town centre.
In Romsey, visit King John's Hunting Lodge, now a heritage centre, and pick up a copy of a town trail to assist your exploration.

7 Return to the Broadlands roundabout and turn left for Winchester. Stay on the A3090, passing a turning on the left for Hillier Gardens. Continue through Ampfield and Hursley, a blend of real and mock-Tudor, to Standon. Now retrace your morning route back into the centre of Winchester.

Old Sarum

This walk explores the Avon Valley and fortified Old Sarum – the massive, deserted ramparts and earthworks set on a bleak hill overlooking modern-day Salisbury (New Sarum). Old Sarum was an important royal and ecclesiastical site, with a castle erected on an earlier Iron Age hill-fort. A cathedral was built inside the castle grounds, but moved to Salisbury in the 13th century.

Route Directions

1 From the car park walk down the access road through the outer bank of the fortified site. Ignore the gates on your left, which give access to the upper and lower ramparts. Proceed through the two gates leading to a waymarked and fenced bridle path and continue along this until you reach a road.

2 Walk through the gate opposite and follow the track ahead. Go past a cottage (Shepherds Corner) and ascend the track. After about 0.25 mile (400m), descend to Keeper's Cottage and arrive at a crossing of paths.

3 Keep straight on, heading uphill and between fields into a wooded area. At a crossing of bridle paths, turn left and walk downhill along a tree-lined path. At a boundary marker, bear right and then continue to a road.

4 Turn left, then after 50yds (46m), turn right down a metalled lane (cul-de-sac). Cross the River Avon and two further footbridges, then follow the metalled path and drive to a road. To get to the The Wheatsheaf turn left. Otherwise, turn right and in 50yds (46m), turn towards the left up a lane.

5 Just before cottages and barns, turn left over a stile and walk down the left-hand field edge, crossing two more stiles and fields. Maintain your direction across the next field, then cross a track and go through the hedge straight ahead of you, then in 100yds (91m) you will reach a stile and road.

6 Cross the road diagonally and take the path down a wooded track. Pass to the left of 'The Bays' to a stile and turn right between the stream and the fence. Cross double stiles in the corner and turn sharp left over another stile, then turn right beside the stream to a white gate and a metalled drive. Turn left and skirt Home Farm and Little Durnford Manor until you get to a gate and a road.

7 Turn right and follow the road for 0.75 mile (1.2km) to a staggered crossroads. Keep ahead towards Stratford sub Castle, crossing the stile on your left in 100yds (91m). Follow the right-hand field edge around the churchyard, cross a stile, a metalled path and a further stile and bear half-right to a gate in the field corner. Head down the next field, pass a barn and cross a stile on to a fenced track.

8 Turn left uphill towards the tree-covered ramparts. Keep left at the junction of paths by a gate, then shortly fork right and steeply climb on to the outer rampart. Turn right and follow the path to a gate and Old Sarum's access road. Turn left back to the car park.

Route facts

DISTANCE/TIME
6 miles (9.7km) 2h

MAP aqua3 OS Explorer 130 Salisbury & Stonehenge

START Old Sarum car park (closes 6pm; 4pm winter), grid ref: SU 139326

TRACKS Footpaths, tracks, bridle paths, stretches of road, 12 stiles

GETTING TO THE START Old Sarum is north of Salisbury off the A345.

THE PUB The Wheatsheaf Inn, Lower Woodford. Tel: 01722 782203

SHAFTESBURY MAP REF ST8723

The idyllic view from the top of Gold Hill in Shaftesbury, with the line of cottages tipping down the steep cobbled road ahead and a perfect panorama to of rolling green Dorset hills behind, is one of the best known in England. You are bound to have seen it before – it is used as the backdrop of many a TV period costume drama, and most famously at the centre of the 1970s Hovis bread advertisements on television, revived in 2006. In fact, thanks in part to the publicity generated by the original Hovis ads, the cobbled road and 700-year-old buttressed abbey walls opposite were given a much needed restoration and make-over in 1980. Today it is a totally pedestrian zone and genuinely charming despite all the hype, though your knees may complain of the steepness after a walk down and back.

The abbey was founded in AD 888, on the edge of Cranborne Chase, by King Alfred for his daughter Aethelgifu and a community of Benedictine nuns. Edward the Martyr, murdered at Corfe Castle, was buried here in 979, making it a very popular (as well as prosperous) site of pilgrimage, and the Danish King Canute insisted that his heart should be interred in the abbey after his death in 1035. In 1539 it was abandoned as part of the dissolution of monasteries that took place across England, and today you can stroll around the low ruins, admire the remains of the Abbey Church, and learn more at the associated museum with its large Anglo Saxon herb garden.

Shaftesbury Town Museum stands at the top of Gold Hill, and celebrates this historic market town which grew fat on the profits of cereals and dairy produce from Cranborne Chase and the near by Blackmore Vale (and the town still fills up for Thursday markets). Traditional Dorsetshire bonnets and button-making were two of the small-scale industries of the town in years gone by.

Just off Bell Street, Swan's Yard is home to many local craftspeople and artists, and is well worth exploring. Another favourite corner is the Pump Yard, near the Olde Two Brewers Inn. It's a delightful little private courtyard of restored houses facing onto St James Street, with an old pump at the centre.

STOCKBRIDGE MAP REF SU3635

Lying deep in the broad Test valley, and spanning that many-streamed river on an artificial causeway constructed in Roman times, Stockbridge consists of a gracious wide street lined with an attractive variety of little houses and shops, with open views eastwards to the hills. It feels as if it should be the main thoroughfare of a sizeable town, but it is not, and behind the elegant façades, the gift and antiques shops, the art galleries and the hotels are the water meadows of the River Test. Some of the river's streamlets, teeming with trout, flow under and alongside the main street.

The most prestigious of English angling clubs, The Houghton, has its headquarters at the Grosvenor Hotel, Stockbridge's most impressive building, with a great pillared porch that juts out into the street and a room above. The town was on a main drovers' route between Wales and Surrey and Kent, and sheep fairs were held here from Tudor times until the early 20th century. Stockbridge Common Marsh is ancient land in the care of the National Trust, as is the open Stockbridge Down, where there is a large Bronze Age cemetery consisting of 15 round barrows.

Northwest of Stockbridge, on the A343, is the Museum of Army Flying at Middle Wallop airfield, which celebrates the history of army aviation. Exhibits include an Argentine Huey helicopter, captured during the Falklands War, and there are hands-on games and activities especially for children.

WINCHESTER MAP REF SU4829

Physically, Winchester is relatively small. Spiritually, emotionally and historically it is large indeed. It was founded shortly before the Romans came, at an important crossing point of the River Itchen. A glance at a map shows how Roman roads radiate from the city like the spokes of a wheel, and certainly Roman Winchester – Venta Belgarum – was as important as this road pattern suggests.

Winchester declined when the Romans left, so that when the shires were created in the 8th century, it did not give its name to the new county. Within a century the situation had been reversed and 'Vintanceastir', as Bede called it, was again ascendant. Alfred the Great made it capital of the West Saxons in AD 871 – Hamo Thorneycroft's statue of him stands at the foot of the High Street – and Winchester remained the capital of Wessex and, in a sense, of England, well into Norman times.

■ Visit

OLD WARDOUR
Northeast of the town, just off the A30 to Salisbury, lies Old Wardour Castle, a romantic ruin in a beautiful landscaped setting. The castle had a unique formation, with a pair of square towers sitting at the entrance and an elegant hexagonal shaped courtyard in the middle. It was started in 1392 as a grand mansion rather than for defence, but was twice besieged during the Civil War, first by Parliamentarians and later by Royalists, and both armies caused such damage that the castle was abandoned. In 1769 New Wardour Castle, a Palladian mansion, was built about 1 mile (1.5km) away.

■ Insight

ST ANN'S GATE
Above St Ann's ancient gateway, built in the 14th century, into the inner city of Salisbury is a small chapel, which became the music room for Malmesbury House. It is said that the great composer Frederick Handel (1685–1759) gave his first public performance in England in this chamber in 1710. The royal coat of arms on the gateway refers to a visit by Charles II in 1665, when he stayed here to avoid an outbreak of plague in London.

■ Insight

FISHING THE TEST
The River Test is famous throughout the world for its trout fishing, which has now become one of the most exclusive leisure pursuits in the country. Fishing above and below Stockbridge town is controlled by two famous – and expensive – clubs, which were founded in the early 19th century and now have waiting lists for its membership. The Leckford Club fishes above the village and the prestigious Houghton Club fishes the 10-mile (16km) stretch below the Leckford water.

The city's prestige began to dwindle once the Treasury moved to London, but the aura of past greatness still lingers and it has been said that Winchester's fine High Street has 'a greater wealth of historical associations than any other street in England'. Here you will find the glorious Buttercross, the Guildhall of 1713 (now a bank) with its overhanging City Clock, the arcaded, timbered row known as the Pentice, and the imposing 14th-century Westgate, a small fortified gateway that once served as a debtors' prison. Explore the little alleyways off here for a feel of the old medieval city – Abbey Passage, just below the Victorian Guildhall, is one of the best.

Winchester Castle, where both kings Henry III and Henry VIII's elder brother, Arthur, were born, was destroyed during the Civil War and only the Great Hall remains. The great round table-top which hangs on the west wall has been linked to King Arthur, but was probably made in Tudor times.

The mighty cathedral does not dominate the city, but sits long and low among the trees and lawns of its lovely close. The present solid, squat Norman building was begun in 1097 by Bishop Wakelin on a floating foundation of logs, for the site was half swamp. In the 14th century Bishop William of Wykeham transformed it into what we see today, replacing the flat roof with great ribs and detailed mouldings, adding tall clustered columns around the original piers, and he introduced vast, spacious, elegant fan vaulting. The cathedral is dedicated to St Swithun (died AD 862), who was bishop here, and his tomb lies

in the cathedral. Also here is the tomb of William II (Rufus) and a plain slab to the novelist, Jane Austen, who died near by in College Street in 1817. Look out for delights such as the richly patterned medieval floor tiles, and a stained-glass window in memory of Izaak Walton, the famous angler. During school term time, evensong is sung by the cathedral choir at 5.30pm, Monday to Saturday, and 3.30pm Sunday. Parts of the cathedral doubled as the Vatican for the 2006 blockbuster movie, *The Da Vinci Code*.

The cathedral close contains part of the priory destroyed by Henry VIII's officers, and the City Museum, while near by lie the ruins of the enormous Bishops' Palace, Wolvesey, largely demolished in 1800. The buildings of Winchester College, England's oldest public school, founded in 1387, lie at the end of College Street, and may be toured. A mile away to the south, and overlooking the River Itchen, you'll find the beautiful Hospital of St Cross – fine almshouses that date from the 12th century, with a fine Norman church and an ancient tradition of providing beer and bread for wayfarers, still given today on request from the porter's lodge.

Winchester is not all history, but is a living city, with excellent shopping, many good museums including a restored water mill, and a lively arts scene.

South of Winchester, Marwell Zoo is a family favourite, with lemurs, monkeys, giraffes, penguins, tigers and more. Free road trains make getting around the vast 100-acre (40.5ha) park easy, and there are animal shows and 'meet the keeper' sessions in summer.

■ TOURIST INFORMATION CENTRES

Romsey
Heritage and Visitor Centre,
Church Street.
Tel: 01794 512987

Salisbury
Fish Row.
Tel: 01722 334956;
www.visitsalisbury.com

Shaftesbury
8 Bell Street.
Tel: 01747 853514;
www.ruraldorset.co.uk

Winchester
The Guildhall, High Street.
Tel: 01962 840500;
www.visitwinchester.co.uk

■ PLACES OF INTEREST

Avington Park
Winchester.
Tel: 01962 779260;
www.avingtonpark.co.uk

Broadlands
Romsey.
Tel: 01794 505010;
www.broadlands.net

Farley Mount Country Park
West of Winchester.
Tel: 01962 860984;
www.hants.gov.uk/countryside

The Grange (EH)
Northington, near Alresford.
Tel: 02392 581059
Free.

Sir Harold Hillier Gardens
Jermyns Lane, Ampfield, by
Romsey.
Tel: 01794 369318;
www.hilliergardens.org.uk

Hospital of St Cross
St Cross Road, Winchester.
Tel: 01962 851375;
www.stcrosshospital.co.uk

King John's House & Tudor Cottage
Church Street, Romsey.
Tel: 01794 512200;
www.romseyheritage.org.uk

Mompesson House (NT)
Cathedral Close, Salisbury.
Tel: 01722 335659

Mottisfont Abbey Garden (NT)
Near Romsey.
Tel: 01794 340575

Museum of Army Flying
Middle Wallop, Stockbridge.
Tel: 01264 784421;
www.flying-museum.org.uk

Old Wardour Castle (EH)
Southwest of Tisbury,
Shaftesbury.
Tel: 01747 870487

Old Sarum (EH)
Castle Road, Salisbury.
Tel: 01722 335398

Redcoats Military Museum
The Wardrobe, Cathedral
Close, Salisbury.
Tel: 01722 419419;
www.thewardrobe.org.uk

Romsey Abbey
Church Place, Romsey.
Tel: 01794 513125

Salisbury & South Wiltshire Museum
The King's House,
65 The Close, Salisbury.
Tel: 01722 332151;
www.salisburymuseum.org.uk

Salisbury Cathedral
Cathedral Close.
Tel: 01722 555120;
www.salisburycathedral.org.uk

Shaftesbury Abbey Museum & Garden
Park Walk, Shaftesbury.
Tel: 01747 852910; www.
shaftesburyabbey.fsnet.co.uk

Shaftesbury Town Museum & Garden
Gold Hill.
Tel: 01747 852157

The Watercress Line
The Railway Station, Station
Road, Alresford.
Tel: 01962 734866;
www.watercressline.co.uk

Wilton House
Wilton, Salisbury.
Tel: 01722 746720;
www.wiltonhouse.co.uk

Winchester Castle & Great Hall
Castle Avenue.
Tel: 01962 846476

Winchester Cathedral
The Close.
Tel: 01962 857200;
www.winchester-
cathedral.org.uk

Winchester City Mill (NT)
Bridge Street, Winchester.
Tel: 01962 870057

Winchester City Museum
The Square, Winchester.
Tel: 01962 848269;
www.winchester.gov.uk

Winchester College tours
College Street, Winchester.
Tel: 01962 621209

■ FOR CHILDREN

Intech – the Family Science Centre
Telegraph Way, Morn Hill.
Tel: 01962 863791;
www.intech-uk.com

Marwell Zoological Park
Colden Common, Winchester.
Tel: 01962 777407;
www.marwell.org.uk
Family-friendly zoo.

■ SHOPPING

Broughton Crafts Ltd
High Street, Stockbridge.
Tel: 01264 810513

Cadogan & James
31A The Square, Winchester.
Tel: 01962 840805;
www. cadoganandcompany.
co.uk
Superb delicatessen.

Fisherton Mill
108 Fisherton Street,
Salisbury.
Tel: 01722 415121;
www.fishertonmill.co.uk
Contemporary art, furniture
and sculpture.

Justice
80 Parchment Street,
Winchester.
Tel: 01962 850890;
www.justice.co.uk
Designer jewellery.

Salisbury
Market Tue and Sat; Farmers'
Markets alternate Weds.

Shaftesbury
Market day, every Thu.

■ PERFORMING ARTS

Chesil Theatre
Chesil Street, Winchester.
Tel: 01962 867086;
www.chesiltheatre.org.uk

Salisbury Playhouse
Malthouse Lane, Salisbury.
Tel: 01722 320333;
www.salisburyplayhouse.com

Theatre Royal
21–23 Jewry Street,
Winchester.
Tel: 01962 840440;
www.theatre-royal-winch
ester.co.uk

■ SPORTS & ACTIVITIES

CYCLE HIRE
Hayball Cyclesport
The Black Horse Chequer,
26–30 Winchester Street,
Salisbury.
Tel: 01722 411378;
www.hayball.co.uk

FISHING
Avington Trout Fishery
Avington Estate, Avington.
Tel: 01962 779312;
www.avingtontrout.com

Broadlands Estate
Broadlands, Romsey.
Tel: 01794 518885

RIDING
Grovely Riding Centre
Water Ditchampton, Wilton,
Salisbury.
Tel: 01722 742288

WALKING
The Itchen Way
A 25-mile (40.2-km) walk
along the River Itchen from
Cheriton to Southampton.

The Test Way
A 44-mile (71km) hike from
Inkpen Beacon to Eling
Wharf.

The Clarendon Way
A 26-mile (42km) trail from
Winchester to Salisbury.

The Avon Valley Path
A 34-mile (55km) route from
Salisbury to Christchurch.

■ ANNUAL EVENTS & CUSTOMS

Alresford
Watercress Festival,
mid-May.

Romsey
Hampshire County Show,
Broadlands Park, end May.
Tel: 01283 820548;
www.livingheritagecountry
shows.co.uk
Romsey Show, Broadlands
Park, early Sep.
Tel: 01794 517521;
www.romseyshow.co.uk

Salisbury
St George's Day. Street
theatre, pageantry and
dragons, 23 Apr.
International Arts Festival.
A variety of art related events
to suit all ages, mid-May to
mid-Jun.

Shaftesbury
Gold Hill Fair, with stalls,
music and dancing. Early Jul.

Winchester
Hat Fair, celebration of street
theatre, late Jun–early Jul.

Tea Rooms

Lillie Langtry's
High Street, Stockbridge, SO20 6HF
Tel: 01264 810954
This old building on the main street was once an inn frequented by actress Lillie Langtry. Today it is a homely tea room, serving crumpets dripping with butter and home-made jam, and scones with clotted cream from a neighbouring Jersey herd. You can also enjoy a light lunch here on the shady terrace by the stream.

Grosvenor Hotel
High Street, Stockbridge, SO20 6EU
Tel: 01264 810606
Enjoy a cream tea, or toasted tea cakes with a choice of different teas and coffees, in the comfort of this grand old fishing hotel, which juts into the High Street.

Miss Moody's Tea Rooms
King John's House, Church Street, Romsey, SO51 8BT
Tel: 01794 512200
With its home-made coffee cake, freshflowers on the tables, friendly service and mismatched floral china teacups, this is surely what a country tea room should be like! Miss Mabel Moody ran a tea room from here in the 1930s, and the tradition continues, with cream teas in summer and light snacks for lunch. There's a pretty courtyard to sit in, too.

Tiffin Tea Rooms
50 West Street, Alresford, SO24 9AU
Tel: 01962 734394
This friendly, traditional tea room with its blue-and-white striped awning serves home-made cakes, cream teas and speciality teas and coffees.

Pubs

The Haunch of Venison
1–5 Minster Street, Salisbury, SP1 1TB
Tel: 01722 411313
Craftsmen working on the cathedral spire were some of the early customers of this pub, dating back to 1320. A restaurant in summer serves treats such as pork with coriander and ginger and coconut Thai *nage*. Beers include Courage Best.

The Mayfly
Testcombe, Stockbridge, SO20 6AZ
Tel: 01264 860283
A lovely old country pub, the Mayfly looks onto the fast-flowing River Test. A selection of hot and cold meats, quiches and pies is laid out buffet-style, along with a few hot daily specials. Beers include Ringwood Best and Wadworth 6X.

The Plough Inn
Main Road, Sparsholt, SO21 2NW
Tel: 01962 776353
Originally the coach house for Sparsholt Manor, the Plough has been tastefully extended over the years and offers a harmonious interior decorated with old farming tools, stone jars and dried hops to complement the real ales and good food on offer. One end of the bar offers light meals such as tomato and olive pasta, and chilli and chickpea cakes with avocado salsa, while the far end offers more serious fare, such as lamb shank.

The Wykeham Arms
75 Kingsgate Street, Winchester, SO23 9PE
Tel: 01962 853834
The 'Wyk', in an old back street near to Winchester College, is a local institution. It is furnished in part with old desks and ephemera from the school. The food is excellent, ranging from the Wyk cottage pie, to grilled sea bass with new potatoes. There is a choice of around 20 wines by the glass, and 60 more by the bottle.

■ TOURIST INFORMATION CENTRES

Bournemouth
Westover Road.
Tel: 0845 051 1700;
www.bournemouth.co.uk

Poole
Enefco House, Poole Quay.
Tel: 01202 253253;
www.pooletourism.com

Swanage
The White House, Shore
Road. Tel: 01929 422885;
www.swanage.gov.uk

Wareham
Holy Trinity Church,
South Street.
Tel: 01929 522740;
www.purbeck.gov.uk

Wimborne
29 High Street.
Tel: 01202 886116;
www.ruraldorset.com

■ OTHER INFORMATION

New Forest Ranger Service
Forestry Commission, The
Queen's House, Lyndhurst.
Tel: 023 8028 6840;
www.forestry.gov.uk/
newforest

Conservation/Heritage organisations
The National Trust (NT)
PO Box 39, Warrington WA5
7WD. Tel: 0870 458 4000;
www.nationaltrust.org.uk

English Heritage (EH)
PO Box 569
Swindon SN2 2YP.
Tel: 0870 333 1181;
www.english-heritage.org.uk

English Nature (EN)
(Hampshire and Isle of Wight
Team) 1 Southampton Road,
Lyndhurst, Hampshire,
SO43 7BU.
Tel: 023 8028 6410;
www.english-nature.org.uk

Royal Society for the Protection of Birds (RSPB)
The Lodge, Sandy,
Bedfordshire SG19 2DL.
Tel: 01767 680551;
www.rspb.org.uk

National Trust (NT)
PO Box 39, Warrington WA5
7WD. Tel: 0870 458 4000;
www.nationaltrust.org.uk

Beaches
Lifeguards are generally
found on busy beaches
during the summer season.
Dogs may not be allowed on
some beaches during busy
summer months.

Coastguard
For Coastguard Assistance
dial 999 and ask for the
Coastguard Service, which
co-ordinates recue services.

Parking
Information on parking
permits and car parks in the
area is available from local
Tourist Information Centres
and on the Web.

Places of Interest
There will be an admission
charge unless stated. For
further information about
specific places or attractions
contact the relevant local TIC
or check on the Web.

Public Transport
Traveline
Tel: 0870 608 2608;
www.traveline.org.uk

Red Funnel Ferries
Town Quay, Southampton
Tel: 0870 444 8898;
www.redfunnel.co.uk

Wight Link Ferries
Tel: 0870 582 774

Hythe Ferry
Tel: 02380 840722;
www.hytheferry.co.uk

Gosport Ferry
Tel: 023 9252 4551;
www.gosportferry.co.uk

Hovertravel
Clarence Esplanade,
Southsea.
Tel: 02392 811000;
www.hovertravel.co.uk

Weather
www.onlineweather.com

■ ORDNANCE SURVEY MAPS

EAST DORSET
Explorer Outdoor Leisure
1:25,000; Sheet 15

NEW FOREST
Explorer Outdoor Leisure
1:25,000; Sheets 22 and 130

ISLE OF WIGHT
Explorer Outdoor Leisure
1:25,000; Sheet 29

PORTSMOUTH & SOUTH EAST COAST
Explorer Outdoor Leisure
1:25,000; Sheets 22 and 119

WINCHESTER & SALISBURY
Explorer Outdoor Leisure
1:25,000; Sheets 130 and 132

The National Grid system covers Great Britain with an imaginary network of grid squares. Each is 100km square in area and is given a unique alphabetic reference, as shown in the diagram above.

These squares are sub-divided into one hundred 10km squares, identified by vertical lines (eastings) and horizontal lines (northings). The reference for the square a feature is located within is made by adding the numbers of the two lines which cross in the bottom left corner of that square to the alphabetic reference (ignoring the small figures). The easting is quoted first. For example, SH6050.

For a 2-figure reference, the zeros are omitted, giving just SH65. In this book, we use 4-figure references, which allow us to pinpoint the feature more accurately by dividing the 10km square into one hundred 1km squares. These squares are not actually printed on the road atlas but are estimated by eye. The same process is carried out as before, giving an enhanced reference of SH6154.

Key to Atlas

M4	Motorway with number		Toll	Toll			Abbey, cathedral or priory		NTS	National Trust for Scotland property
S Fleet	Motorway service area			Road underconstruction			Aquarium			Nature reserve
	Motorway toll			Narrow Primary route with passing places			Castle			Other place of interest
1	Motorway junction with and without number			Steep gradient			Cave		P·R	Park and Ride location
3	Restricted motorway junctions			Railway station and level crossing			Country park			Picnic site
	Motorway and junction under construction			Tourist railway			County cricket ground			Steam centre
A3	Primary route single/dual carriageway			National trail			Farm or animal centre			Ski slope natural
BATH	Primary route destinations			Forest drive			Garden			Ski slope artifical
	Roundabout			Heritage coast			Golf course			Tourist Information Centre
Y 5 Y	Distance in miles between symbols			Ferry route			Historic house			Viewpoint
A1123	Other A Road single/dual carriageway		6	Walk start point			Horse racing			Visitor or heritage centre
B2070	B road single/dual carriageway		1	Cycle start point			Motor racing			Zoological or wildlife collection
	Unclassified road single/dual carriageway		3	Tour start point			Museum			Forest Park
	Road tunnel						Airport			National Park (England & Wales)
							Heliport			
							Windmill			National Scenic Area (Scotland)
						NT	National Trust property			

Page numbers in bold refer to main entries.

A
Ackling Dyke 31
Albert, Prince Consort 84, 96
Alfred the Great, King 144, 145
Alresford **132**, 134–5
Alum Bay **88**
Ampfield **133**
Appuldurcombe House 92
Arlott, John 132
Arne 42–3
Arthur, King 131, 147
Ashurst **54**
Athelhampton 42
Austen, Jane 118, 138, 147
Avington Park **133**
Avon, River 57, 60, 62, 70, 138
Avon Valley Path 70
Awdry, Rev W 133

B
Badbury Rings 31
Bank 72–3
Barry, Sir Charles 31
beach huts 24
Beaulieu 10, 50, **54–5**
Beaulieu River 57, 62
Bembridge **88–9**
Blackmore Vale 144
Boleyn, Anne 116
Botley **112**
Bournemouth 20, 23, **24–5**
Bovington **25**
Brading **89**
Breamore **55**
Brickfields Horse Country 93
Broadlands 137
Brockenhurst **55**
Brown, 'Capability' 33, 92, 137
Brydges, George 133
Buckler's Hard **57**
Burley **57**, 58–9
Burne-Jones, Edward 69
Bursledon 113, 114–15
Burt, George 41

C
Calbourne **89**
Calshot 9, **57**
Cameron, Julia Margaret 92
Canute, King 144
Carisbrooke Castle 87, **91**, 92
Carnarvon, Margaret,
    Marchioness of 133
Carroll, Lewis 70
Charles I, King 87, 89
Charles II, King 99, 117, 133,
    145
Chettle 29
Chichester Harbour 113
Christchurch 10, 53, **60**
Civil War 23, 29, 145, 147
Clouds Hill 25
Cobbett, William 112, 133
Compton Acres 34
Constable, John 138
Corfe Castle 23, 26–7, **29**
Cort, Henry 112
Cowes 87, **91**, 94–5
Cranborne Chase 20, 23, **29–30**,
    144
Cubitt, Thomas 96
cycling 17

D
D-Day Museum, Southsea 119
Damer, Joseph and Caroline 33
Dickens, Charles 117
Dolls House, Lulworth 32
Domesday Book 60, 62, 112
Dorset, East 18–47
Double Dikes 60
Doyle, Sir Arthur Conan 70
Durdle Door 9, 23, 32, 36–7
Durleston Castle, Swanage 41

E
Edward II, King 29
Edward the Martyr, King 29,
    144
Eling **60–2**
Emery Down 70
Ethelred II the Unready, King 29

Euridice (ship) 97
Exbury House **62**

F
Fareham **112**
Farley Mount **136**
Farmer Palmer's, Sandford 43
Fine Foundation Marine Centre
    31
flying boats 55, 57, 118
Fontmell Down 29
Fordingbridge **62–3**
Forster, John and Alfred 62
Fort Victoria Country Park 99
Fossil Forest 32
Freshwater 87, **91–2**, 100–1
Fritham **63**, 64–5
Furzey Gardens 53, 70

G
George IV, King 133
Godshill **92**
Gosport 117
Graves, Robert 97

H
Hamble 31, **113**, 114–15
Handel, George Frederick 145
Hardy, Thomas 20
Hayling Island **113**
Henry I, King 60, 63, 116
Henry III, King 147
Henry V, King 116
Henry VIII, King 53, 57, 63, 69,
    99, 116–17, 147
Highcliffe Castle 53
Hillier Gardens 131, 133
Hockey's Farm 63
Hurst Castle 53, 69

I
Isle of Wight 82–105
Isle of Wight Steam Railway 93
Itchen, River 145, 147

J
John, Augustus 63
John, King 29, 137, 138
Johnson, Gerard 119
Jurassic Coast 20

K
Keats, John 97
Keble, John 24, 133
Kennington, Eric 42
Kimmeridge Bay **30–1**
Kingston Lacy 23, **31**
Kipling, John Lockwood 96
Knightwood Oak 55, 72–3
Knoll Gardens 43
L
Langstone Harbour 108, 113, 119
Lawrence, T E (Lawrence of Arabia) 20, 25, 42
Leighton, Lord 70
Lepe Country Park 57
Liberty's Raptor and Reptile Centre 71
Lilliput Museum of Antique Dolls and Toys, Brading 89
Linwood 66–7
Longdown Activity Farm 54
Lulworth Cove 9, 23, **32**, 36–7
Lymington 53, **69**, 99
Lyndhurst 54, **69–70**
M
Malmesbury House 145
Manor Farm Country Park 112
Marconi, Guglielmo 88
Marwell Zoo 147
Mary Rose (ship) 116–17
Medina, River 91, 92
Melbury Down 29
Milne, A A 97
Milton Abbas **33**
Minstead **70**
Mitford, Mary Russell 132
Mompesson House 138
Monkey World 32
Monmouth, Duke of 71
Montagu, Lord 54
Moors Valley Country Park 71
Moreton 25
Morley, Richard 133
Morton Manor, Brading 89

Mottisfont **136**
Mottisfont Abbey 136
Mottistone Manor Garden 89
Mountbatten, Lord 137
Museum of Army Flying 145
N
Nash, John 92
National Motor Museum 50, 54–5
The Needles 9, 41, 84, 87, 88, 91
Nelson, Lord 57, 116
Netley **116**
Netley Abbey 111, 116
New Forest 48–81
New Forest Otter, Owl and Wildlife Conservation Park 54
New Forest Reptile Centre 70
New Forest Visitor Centre and Museum 70
Newport **92**, 94–5
Newtown **93**
Nightingale, Florence 137
Northington Grange 132
Nunwell House 89
O
Old Sarum 131, 136, 137, 142–3
Old Wardour Castle 145
Osborne House 84, **93**, 96, 97
P
Palmerston, Lord 137
Parkhurst Forest 93
ponies, New Forest 54
Poole **33–4**
Poole Harbour 23, 33, 38–9, 42, 43
Poole Pottery 34
Portchester Castle **116**
Ports Down 120–1
Portsmouth 9, 11, 108, **116–17**
Portsmouth Harbour 113, 116, 117
Priest's House Museum, Wimborne Minster 43
Purbeck, Isle of 29, 32, 38–9

Purbeck Hills 20, 29
Purbeck Way 26
Q
Quarr Abbey 93
R
Red House Museum, Christchurch 60
Rhinefield Ornamental Drive 55
Ringwood **70–1**
Rockbourne **71**, 76–7
Romans 31, 71, 76, 89, 92–3, 116, 145
Romsey **136–7**, 140–1
Romsey Abbey 137
Rosemary Vineyard 93
Rothschild, Lionel de 62
Royal Navy Submarine Museum, Gosport 117
Royal Victoria Country Park 116
Rufus Stone 63
Russell-Cotes Art Gallery and Museum, Bournemouth 25
Ryde **96**
S
St Barbe Museum, Lymington 69
Salisbury 131, **137–8**, 140–1
Salisbury Cathedral 29, 131, 137
Sandbanks 33, 34
Sandown 9, **96**
Seaview **96–7**
Shaftesbury 29, **144**
Shakespeare, William 119
Shalfleet 93
Shanklin **96**, 99
Shanklin Chine 10, 87, 96
Shelley, John 133
Shelley, Mary 24
Shelley, Percy Bysshe 24
Silver Route 136
Smedmore House 30
Smuggling Museum, Ventnor 99
Soldier Brothers' Memorial 62

Solent 50, 84, 93, 108, 113
Solent Sky Aviation Museum
  118
Solent Way 119
South West Coast Path 32
Southampton 108, 113, **118**
Southampton, 1st Earl of 119
Southampton Water 55, 60–2,
  113
Southeast Coast 106–25
Southsea 108, 117, **118–19**
Southwick 120–1
Spinnaker Tower, Portsmouth
  9, 111, 116
Spinners 69
Spithead 93, 119
Stapehill 43
Stockbridge 140–1, **144–5**
Stour, River 43, 60
Studland Bay 11, 20, **34**
Studland Museum and Heritage
  Centre 41
Swan Green 70

Swanage **41**
Swein 89
Swithun, St 147
T
Tank Museum, Bovington 25
Tennyson, Alfred Lord 87, 91–2
Tennyson Down 88
Tennyson Trail 88
Test, River 136, 144, 145
Thackeray, William 112
Thomas, Cecil 62
Titchfield **119**
Titchfield Haven 108
Tolpuddle **41–2**
Tolpuddle Martyrs 20, 41–2
Tyneham 31
V
Ventnor **97–9**
Victoria, Queen 84, 91
Victory, HMS 116
W
walking 16
Walton, Izaak 147

Wareham 33, **42–3**
watercress 132
Watercress Line 131, 132
Whistler, Lawrence 25
Whistler, Rex 136
White Moor Heath 70
Whitsbury Manor Stud 71
Wilfred, St 89
William II Rufus, King 63, 147
William IV, King 91
William the Conqueror 30, 50,
  63, 69, 131, 137
Wilton House 138
Wimborne Minster **43**
Winchester 128, 131, 140–1,
  145–7
Winterborne Clenston 33
Worbarrow Bay 32
Worth Matravers 29
Wren, Christopher 32, 41
Wyatt, James 138
Y
Yarmouth **99**, 100–1

The Automobile Association would like to thank the following photographers and companies for their assistance in the preparation of this book. Abbreviations for the picture credits are as follows – (t) top; (b) bottom; (c) centre; (l) left; (r) right; (AA) AA World Travel Library

Front cover AA/A Burton; inside front cover AA/A Burton; back cover AA/A Burton; inside back cover flap AA/M Moody; back cover flap (i) AA/A Burton; (ii) AA/M Jourdan; (iii) AA/A J Hopkins; (iv) AA/A Burton; (v) AA/W Voysey; (vi) AA/J A Tims; 1 AA/A Burton; 4 AA/A Burton; 7 AA/A Burton; 8t AA/M Jourdan; 8bl AA/A Burton; 8cr AA/A Burton; 9 AA/S McBride; 10t AA/A Burton; 10c AA/A Burton; 10b AA/A Burton; 11t AA/A Burton; 11b AA/W Voysey; 13 AA/A Burton; 14 AA/S Day; 18bl AA/A Burton; 18br AA/A Burton; 19 AA/A Burton; 21tl AA/A Burton; 21tr AA/A Burton; 21c AA/R Ireland; 21b AA/A Burton; 22tl AA/A Burton; 22tr AA/A Burton; 22b AA/M Jourdan; 23t AA/P Enticknap; 23c AA/J A Tims; 23b AA/A Burton; 28 AA/J A Tims; 35 AA/A Burton; 40 AA/A Burton; 46 AA/A Burton; 48bl AA/A Burton; 48br AA/A Burton; 49 AA/A J Hopkins; 51t AA/A Burton; 51bl AA/W Voysey; 51br AA/A Burton; 52cl AA/A Burton; 52cr AA/A Burton; 52b AA/A Burton; 53t AA/A Burton; 53c AA/A Burton; 53b AA/A Burton; 56 AA/A Burton; 61 AA/A Burton; 68 AA/A Burton; 74/75 AA/A Burton; 80 AA/A Burton; 82bl AA/S McBride; 82br AA/A Burton; 83 AA/A Burton; 85tl AA/A Burton; 85tr AA/A Burton; 85br AA/A Burton; 86c AA/A Burton; 86b AA/A Burton; 86b AA/A Burton; 87t AA/A Burton; 87c AA/A Burton; 87b AA/A Burton; 90 AA/A Burton; 98 AA/A Burton; 104 AA/S McBride; 106l AA/A Burton; 106r AA/S & O Matthews; 107 AA/A Burton; 109t AA/W Voysey; 109b AA/W Voysey; 110 AA/A Burton; 111t AA/D Croucher; 111b AA/A Burton; 124 AA/A Burton; 126bl AA/M Moody; 126br AA/M Moody; 127 AA/J A Tims; 128 AA/M Moody; 129t AA/A Burton; 129b AA/J A Tims; 130cr AA/M Moody; 130br AA/J A Tims; 131t AA/M Moody; 131b AA/M Moody; 139 AA/J A Tims; 146 AA/M Moody; 150 AA/J A Tims

Every effort has been made to trace the copyright holders, and we apologise in advance for any accidental errors. We would be happy to apply the corrections in the following edition of this publication.